D1616497

THE HANLON BROTHERS

THE HANLON BROTHERS

*Their Amazing Acrobatics, Pantomimes
and Stage Spectacles*

John A. McKinven

David Meyer ⋅✕⋅ Magic Books

GLENWOOD, ILLINOIS · 1998

ISBN 0-916638-82-0

This book was designed by Dan Franklin and composed
by Village Typographers, Inc., of Belleville, Illinois.

LIBRARY OF CONGRESS CATALOGING-IN-PUBLICATION DATA

McKinven, John A. (John Alexander), 1920–
    The Hanlon Brothers : their amazing acrobatics, pantomimes,
and stage spectacles / John A. McKinven.
        p.   cm.
    Includes bibliographical references.
    ISBN 0-916638-82-0 (alk. paper)
    1. Hanlon-Lees (Theatrical troupe).   2. Entertainers—Great
Britain—Biography.   I. Title.
PN2599.5.T54M38   1998
791′.092′241—dc21
[B]
                                                            97-52994
                                                            CIP

David Meyer ⁖ Magic Books

is an imprint of
Meyerbooks, Publisher
235 West Main Street, Box 427
Glenwood, Illinois 60425

Contents

Illustrations

PATENT DRAWINGS

COLOR ILLUSTRATIONS
following page 66

An Important Note to the Reader

In the last half of the 19th century there was hardly a name in the amusement world better known than the Hanlon Brothers. As breathtaking acrobats they dazzled audiences in every part of the world. As superb pantomimists they were the hit of two continents and laid the groundwork for many comedians of the silent screen. As producers they created and acted in giant pantomimic spectacles which played to packed houses and occasionally broke box office records in America's largest theatres.

And yet, their accomplishments have received scanty notice in American theatrical literature. This book is an attempt to recapture details of the Hanlons' many-faceted career and how it evolved.

There are several personal objectives behind the work:

An appreciable amount of the details I wish to preserve has come from newspaper clippings which are moldering away. One difficulty has been the number of clippings in scrapbooks and private files which have been carefully trimmed, thereby eliminating the name of the newspaper and/or the date.

As far as possible, I have adhered to a chronological sequence as a help to students who may in the future want to fill in some of the gaps and correct errors.

Above all, it was my desire to get a better appreciation of what audiences at a Hanlon performance actually saw on the stage.

Finally, one very important clarification of the Hanlon story is offered here. In order to follow the story and understand the relationships among the six brothers, it is essential to know their ages and positions in the family. I have found that almost every biographical sketch or newspaper article which states their ages is in error. This is particularly true of George and William. Some of the confusion has been caused by an 1881 article in the *New York Clipper* which misstated their birth years when they arrived in this country with *Le Voyage en Suisse*. The errors have been copied over and over. The author of the article, Col. T. Allston Brown, repeated the incorrect dates in his three-volume work *A History of the New York Stage* (1903). More mix-up was the result of George and William's frequently giving erroneous ages when interviewed, a practice they were still following as late as 1921. Consequently, what little biographic data is in print must puzzle a researcher. For example, the ages of George, William and Alfred when they set off on their first world tour were not "four to eight" but were actually 11, 7 and 4 years, respectively.

Fortunately, Mother Hanlon saw to it that the boys were properly baptized. The Hanlon brothers' order of birth and the correct dates as recorded in the baptismal archives of the Cathedral in Manchester, England, together with the dates of their deaths from newspaper obituaries, are:

Thomas	March ?, 1833–April 5, 1868
George	October 10, 1835–November 5, 1926
William	November 7, 1839–February 7, 1923
Alfred[1]	1842–January 24, 1886
Edward	August 31, 1845–March 9, 1931
Frederick[2]	1848–April 6, 1886

According to the church records, all the natural brothers were born in Manchester except Edward, who was born in Liverpool. The records also reveal an older brother, Robert, who was born in February 1831. We know that he survived at least to the age of 8, when he was baptized. In *Mémoires et Pantomimes des Frères Hanlon-Lees* (Paris, 1880), Robert, Henry and a sister are mentioned as siblings who "lived only a few years."

The father of the boys, Thomas Hanlon, was said to be the manager of a Manchester theatre. He married Ellen Hughes on October 4, 1830, and the *Mémoires* mentions a fiftieth anniversary celebration being planned in 1879. The sons' baptism entries list their parents' occupation as "bookkeepers" or "accountants." Thomas Senior was born in 1811 and died on November 7, 1880.

Acknowledgments and Sources

The first ten years were an epic journey. Three very small boys and a young adult leader took ten years to circle the globe and visit many countries at a time when travel and living conditions were often primitive. They had numerous trials and adventures.

One source for the story of these travels is *Mémoires et Pantomimes des Frères Hanlon-Lees,* published in Paris in 1880, about 30 years after the tour. The *Mémoires* appeared during the Hanlons' great successes in pantomime for Parisian audiences. The text takes the form of an interview with Richard Lesclide and a lengthy preface by Theodore De Banville, a noted poet. Illustrations are by Frederic Regamey. The story is sketchy and romantic. Large portions of the Hanlons' history as acrobats are omitted. The purpose of the book was undoubtedly promotion for the pantomimists, who at the time were headliners in Paris theatres and were highly acclaimed by French intellectuals.

To augment this, there are a handful of newspaper clippings in which one or another of the Hanlons tells and retells the stories in later years. Inevitably there are discrepancies. No doubt some of the young travelers' adventures were embroidered to increase the drama. For example, one anecdote in the *Mémoires* is probably apocryphal. A story about a performance before the Sultan's harem has appeared in biographies of Gustave Fratellini, Jean Gaspard, Debureau and others.[1] But perhaps Alfred Hanlon did indeed emerge from the seraglio with a large diamond ring on his thumb.

By judiciously (I hope) merging some of the *Mémoires* and later interviews, I have tried to produce a plausible account of the first ten years. In any event, the scenarios for the earlier pantomimes included in the *Mémoires* are valuable insights into the sight gags and mad, pantomimic humor of the Hanlons.

For most of the book, I have depended mainly upon playbills, programs and newspaper interviews and reviews to supply the story. For the original batch of newspaper clippings I must thank Burtram Platt at the Cohasset (Massachusetts) Historical Society.

In the beginning the impetus to research the Hanlons came from Jay Marshall, with whom I shared a great curiosity about this legendary but obscure team. Over the years he has provided many excerpts from his library and at one point spent hours searching microfilm to collect Chicago advertisements for Hanlon shows. Jay never failed to bring me back to the Hanlons when other interests intervened.

An early bonanza came from Ricky Jay, who sent two pages of references because, in his encyclopedic researches into show business oddities, he too was accumulating material on the Hanlons. I am especially grateful for his permission to reproduce the posters illustrated in Plates 4, 6 and 7 from his collection. It was he who arranged a wonderful afternoon visiting with Dr. Laurence Senelick of Tufts University and dipping into his collection of Hanlon material.

Another Hanlon enthusiast, John Towsen, author of *Clowns,* very generously supplied valuable background files from his own work on the Hanlons. His story of the Hanlon-Lees as it appears in his book is one of the best accounts currently available.

In preparing the manuscript, I was very grateful for the editorial suggestions and the meticulous proofreading of Mary Parrish.

Along the way there are many others who have provided pieces of the mosaic. Among them are Claude Crowe, Mike Caveney, Edwin Dawes, Tom Ewing, John Fisher, the late Ed Freeman, James Hamilton, David Meyer, Jim Steinmeyer and David Sigafus. I thank them all and apologize to anyone I have inadvertently omitted.

Important sources as noted in the credits have been:

The Harvard Theatre Collection, Houghton Library, Cambridge, Massachusetts

The New York Public Library for the Performing Arts, Lincoln Center, New York City

The Library of Congress, Washington, D.C., Film Archive Center

Governor State University, Governors Park, Illinois (microfilm file of *The New York Clipper*)

The Boston Public Library, Rare Books Department

Northern Illinois University, DeKalb (microfilm file of *The New York Mirror*)

THE HANLON BROTHERS

⌒

CHAPTER ONE

The First Ten Years
Around the World

It was a thoroughly theatrical family.

The father, Tom Hanlon, Senior, had originally studied for the ministry but abandoned that to become an itinerant actor, playing mostly in comedies. While on tour, Tom met and married a fellow player, Ellen Hughes, a Welsh woman. When children began to arrive, he settled down and became theatre manager of the Manchester Theatre Royale. The children were "born under the gleam of gas footlights in the shadow of forests of cloth and cardboard."[1]

Tom, the eldest living son, took up gymnastics early and became proficient enough to be engaged as an instructor. All the boys who followed became acrobats and gymnasts.

William recalled that he made his first appearance in a Liverpool theatre at about the age of six in the show of the magician M. Jacobs, a competitor of John Henry Anderson. William was to emerge from the covers of an enormous book. But hiding beneath a table, he fell asleep, missed his cue and was dragged from his place of concealment to the shouts of a laughing audience.[2]

By the time Edward was on the way, the family table was very crowded. As George commented many years later, "We are originally Irish and God who blesses big families gave us a particular blessing. . . . One knows that in fairy tales when families become very numerous, the father, after a long discussion with the mother, arises very early and goes to lose a party of kids in the woods. That is known as the Tom Thumb fairy tale. Fortunately our parents loved us more than that tradition."[3] They preferred to hand over their children to someone of good repute for training, education and a vocation.

As fate would have it, John Lees, a friend of the boys' father, appeared with a proposal. Lees, from a good family, was educated as a gentleman and was also a clever gymnast. He had a burning desire to see the world and thought an acrobatic act modeled after the then-new act of Professor Risley and Sons would be the ticket. The Risley act, coming from America, consisted of the performer lying on his back with legs in the air, juggling young child tumblers with his feet. It is an impressive feat that is still occasionally seen today.

Lees proposed that George, William and Alfred be apprenticed to him for training, and the parents consented. Practice began almost immediately. The young boys, at least George and William, had watched their older brother Tom and already knew some of the rudiments of gymnastics. With a minimum of rehearsal, Lees and his infant troupe began a series of out-of-town trial openings.

On July 12, 1846, "Professor Lees and his Infant Pupil" were on the bill at The Victoria Temple in Edinburgh (allegedly coming from Cooke's Royal Amphitheatre). By August 12, "Mr. Lees and his talented pupil Master George" were appearing at the Edinburgh Adelphi Theatre, and for the next two weeks it was "Master George and Master Alfred 3½ Years Old."[4] Apparently, William was not yet ready.

On Boxing Day, December 26, Professor John Lees and his Three Pupils, The Masters Hanlon, billed as "The Celebrated Entortilationists,"[5] appeared at the Theatre Adelphi in London. It was the formal debut of George, William and Alfred and their entry into the "big time." They were 11, 7 and 4 years of age. The act was a success and stayed at the Adelphi until February 6, 1847.

Eager to travel, Lees took his troupe to Paris. There they found a number of competitors doing the Risley act, so Lees cast about for something to distinguish his version. He signed an engagement with the Hippodrome and began work on a grand rolling carriage to travel around the arena and show off the act in motion.

Lees wanted to visit lesser-known countries. France was unsettled with economic problems and the Revolution of 1847 under way. After a short tour, mostly as strolling players, the group crossed the frontier into Spain. Travel became much more arduous. There were no railroads, and the troupe often made its way on pack mules. Spain was in a civil war, and the mountains were full of bandits and rival brigands. The *Mémoires* contain tales of dangerous encounters and escapes. More than once, Lees was forced to fend off thugs, sometimes with his pistol.

In contrast, when the troupe arrived in Madrid, they found an animated, lively community seemingly unaffected by the strife. Lees' group opened in the Madrid Circus and became social lions . . . little lions. Such a group of entertainers was quite out of the ordinary. Each of the boys wore a Scottish uniform with a national scarf, the legs bare, and the sporan of Highlanders.

A Court Ball was being held in Madrid, and such affairs were often dull. Mr. Lees and his troupe were invited to relieve the monotony. They did, and from that

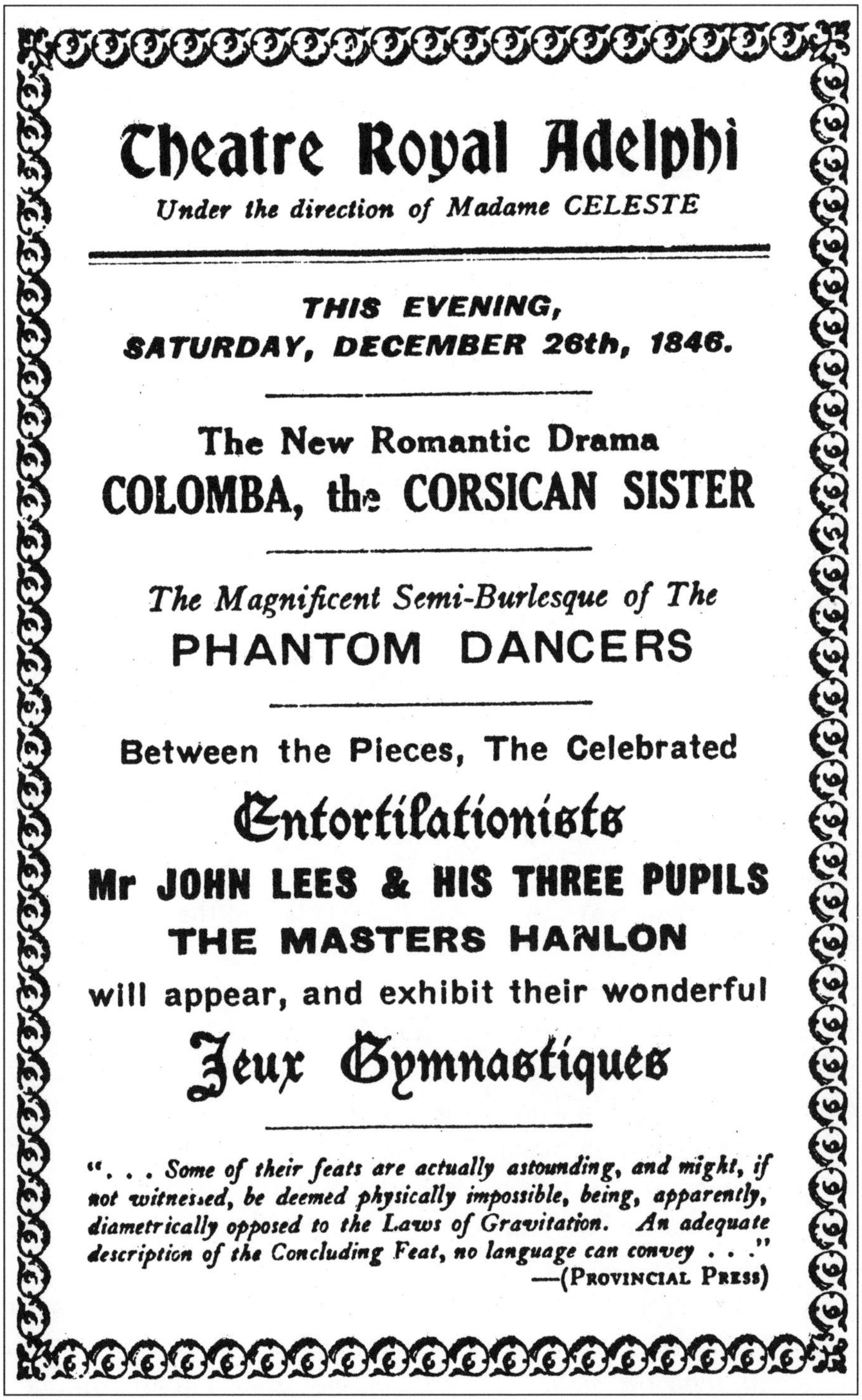

Theatre Royal Adelphi
Under the direction of Madame CELESTE

THIS EVENING,
SATURDAY, DECEMBER 26th, 1846.

The New Romantic Drama
COLOMBA, the CORSICAN SISTER

The Magnificent Semi-Burlesque of The
PHANTOM DANCERS

Between the Pieces, The Celebrated
Entortilationists
Mr JOHN LEES & HIS THREE PUPILS
THE MASTERS HANLON
will appear, and exhibit their wonderful
Jeux Gymnastiques

". . . Some of their feats are actually astounding, and might, if not witnessed, be deemed physically impossible, being, apparently, diametrically opposed to the Laws of Gravitation. An adequate description of the Concluding Feat, no language can convey . . ."
—(Provincial Press)

Figure 1. Playbill for the formal debut of John Lees and his pupils, George, William and Alfred Hanlon, on December 26, 1846, in "Entortilationists." (From *Life and Letters Today*, April 1841.)

time they were the rage in Spain. There was an abundance of party invitations from noble ladies.

The boys were exceptionally attractive. In their kilts they had the appearance of young girls in short skirts, especially William, with his big eyes and curly hair. The young ladies called him "señorita" and brought him presents of dolls. One day in a moment of anger, forgetting he had nothing under his kilt, he rebelled and turned a somersault which dispelled any notion that he was a girl. Lees saw to it that thereafter the boys were dressed as dandies—short and tight trousers, silk stockings, vests with glitter and a Spanish cap.

Two very pretty girls, ladies of the court, led in making much of the boys. One was Eugenie de Montijo, Countess of Theba, a 21-year-old blonde, and the other her sister, the Duchess of Alba, a dark-haired Spanish beauty. Eugenie particularly took a fancy to William, then about 9. He was equally taken by her pair of spirited Arabian ponies and enjoyed many a daredevil ride with Eugenie handling the reins. Eugenie later married Louis Napoleon (Napoleon III) and became Empress of France.

Eugenie and her sister saw to it that the boys had an audience with Queen Isabella. In spite of rigorous coaching beforehand on how to remove their hats and kneel before kissing the hand, George failed to take off his cap. The Queen, impressed by William's good behavior, took him in her lap and kissed him.

For three years Lees and his boys journeyed through Spain from city to city and from one grandee's *casa* to another. With the aptitude of bright youths they picked up the language quickly.

Sailing through Gibraltar, the group stopped at Malta and then travelled on to Greece, Turkey, Egypt and India.

As guardian and teacher, Lees proved to be an ideal leader for the children, and they loved him dearly. In an interview 30 years later, George summed up his regard: "For us Lees was not simply a professor but a devoted protector, a second father. Other than being an able gymnast, he had a big heart and combined a practical sense toward life with an inclination toward little fantasies. Artist and man of affairs at the same time, his fatherly severities were tempered to the liveliness of children. He encouraged our education, our self-respect and saw to our moral and physical education, not like a master but as a great friend."[6]

Lees was also an able protector. In Greece, a nasty troublemaker with a knife in his belt insisted on entering the theatre without a ticket. Lees said no. When the Greek lunged with the knife, he missed. Lees stepped aside and hit him flush in the face, ending the matter.

After playing at Constantinople for a time, Lees and his boys were engaged to show off their skills before Her Highness at the palace. This was a great honor, and the young men were jubilant, hoping that the audience would include the Sultan's harem.

On one side of the palace room was a narrow mesh grill, impossible to see through. Behind that mysterious partition were the flowers of the harem, gathered to watch the acrobats.

When the show concluded, the invisible audience was so very delighted that a eunuch appeared to announce that the favorite Sultana, with the permission of Her Highness, desired to compliment Monsieur Lees. John Lees' momentary anticipation was dashed when the servant explained that on the begging of the women, the august Caliph permitted only one of the troupe near them . . . the smallest of the M. Lees.

Alfred, then about 8, accompanied the eunuch, and after a visit with the sultanas, emerged with a superb, brilliant diamond on his thumb.

Arriving at Alexandria, Lees found no suitable theatre in the city and decided there was a fortune to be made. He had a theatre built at his expense. Opening night was a great success, but the next night no one came. The Alexandrians had seen one performance, and that was sufficient. The theatre was a failure and was the beginning of a streak of bad luck. They moved to Cairo and built another theatre, the first one in Cairo, only to have a repetition of the same experience. "There isn't five cents worth of curiosity in the country," said George later.[7]

As consolation, they decided to visit the pyramids and set off for the Great Pyramid at Gizeh. They missed the boat on the Nile and completed the trip partly riding on burros and partly walking on shifting sands. It was an arduous journey, with exhausted children sometimes having to be carried. They did finally reach the pyramid and climbed to the top. Again missing the boat, they had a long, weary trip ahead. When they arrived back at Cairo, the town gates were locked and they spent the night on the bare ground.

All of this was roses compared to what was in store. Several days later, as the troupe rehearsed their routines in the theatre, thieves entered their rooms and stole Lees' chest, which contained 100,000 francs and innumerable gifts they had received. It was the fruit of several years of hard work, and the theft left them practically penniless. They desperately wanted to get out of Egypt and on to India.

Appeals to the local authorities were fruitless, but the resident British envoy took pity on his countrymen and used his friendship to secure an exhibition before Abbas-Pasha, the rich and powerful khedive who ruled at Dab el Bekah, an oasis on the road between Cairo and Suez.

Abbas was delighted with the stunts of the foreigners and kept them almost three weeks, performing nightly. In turn he treated them to mock but bloody battles between his soldiers using javelins and troupes of Arabs on horseback. The Pasha was generous and paid the entertainers handsomely in money and gifts, more than enough to get to India.

As they were embarking at Suez on the steamer "Indostany," their trip was marred by a serious shipboard fire, but it was brought under control. After putting in at Aden, they steamed the 2,000 miles to India and began a happy stay of two years.

The coastal cities of Calcutta, Madras and Bombay could be reached by ship and, being British towns, they gave the acrobats a warm welcome. After a time, they began to receive invitations from the interior, where rajahs governed under the British protectorate. The rajahs were rich and eager for foreign entertainment.

Traveling inland was much more arduous. The troupe was sometimes afoot, sometimes carried through jungles in palanquins. There were no railroads, and the group reached Mysore in primitive wagons with no semblance of comfort. The nearby town of Seringpatam had been the fortress of Tipoo-Sahib, a rebel leader who had built a broad moat stocked with crocodiles as defense. The Rajah of Mysore had aided the British in capturing the town, but the moat and its inhabitants stayed. When the boys arrived at four or five o'clock in the morning, dirty and tired, the moat looked like an inviting pond for a swim and they very nearly dove in before a sentry told them of the danger. They were warmly received by the Rajah of Mysore, but their stay was shortened because the cholera season came on and the boys fled north.[8]

For all the trials, there were sights and experiences to last Lees and the boys for the rest of their lives. Along the way the trees were sometimes filled with swarming monkeys for what seemed like hundreds of miles. At one place, scorpions rained down from the place where their trapeze was fixed. They played at a palace made entirely from sandalwood, which gave out a perfume like the fans that ladies carry.

The Rajah of Oudh took a fancy to the boys, dressed them like princes and kept them for an extended time. The Rajah was a chess fanatic and had a hall wholly devoted to the game. William could play chess with some skill, and Lees announced that the boy was a chess wonder-worker and boldly issued a challenge to the court to name a champion to meet him.

The Rajah was all curiosity. Nothing was talked about in the court except the great chess match to come. William felt terrible. He had seen the court champion—a bearded, six-foot Mohammedan with a turban that added to his height.

For a week William worried over chess problems. With the whole court looking on, the match began. When the boy was finally checkmated, the courtiers let out a sigh of relief. As for the Rajah, he was so pleased that his man had won that he decorated William with a gold chain.

The rajahs, nabobs and princes of India proved to be a bonanza for the touring entertainers. By the end of their tour they had accumulated deluxe guns, cashmere shawls, an exquisite ivory chess set and a greater variety of elaborate Indian artwork than they could carry.

After passing through Java and Singapore for short stays, they proceeded to Australia, where the gold fever was at its height. Melbourne was mad with excitement, and the mud was ankle deep. During the first gold rush there were at one time 400 sailing vessels in the harbor with not a soul aboard. In their wild desire for gold, the men had all deserted and gone to the mines.[9]

William later described the scene:

> The Boll and Mouth tavern usually had men from the mines standing three deep at the bar waiting to be served. They generally threw down a small gold nugget for their drink, seldom waiting for any change. Men hitherto penniless had struck it rich and their sudden streak of luck turned their heads. One would light his pipe with a five pound note and another not to be outdone would put a ten pound note between two slices of bread and butter and eat it. Four sailors from the mines at dinner one night set up quart bottles of champagne in the form of ten pins at one end of a long table. Then standing at the opposite end of the table they would hurl bottles of wine at the ten pins keeping the waiters resetting the pins. The first tier of boxes at the theatre were generally filled with rough miners, their legs dangling over the box rails, while bottles were passed from box to box. If anything in the performance appealed to the auditors, the roars of bravos which exploded on our heads were terrific. The entire theatre burst with enthusiasm which converted into a rain of gold nuggets scattered on the stage of our circus, more productive than the placers.[10]

All the world, it seemed, headed for the placers. After six months in Melbourne and Sydney, the group was caught up in the fever and started for the mines in wagons. The fields were between Bendigo and Ballarat, 75 to 100 miles from Melbourne. They anticipated difficulties finding theatres suitable for their shows, so they carried heavy equipment followed by six Indian servants and an immense tent. They didn't erect it in cities but near the mines where the wealthy gathered. In 1852, gold fever and dreams of riches affected everyone. The performers could not retain the servants even after assuring them a considerable salary.

The great wealth and riotous living also attracted a horde of convicts and thugs, who killed and robbed to enrich themselves without working. More than once Lees and his boys ran into rough situations. Usually their superb gymnastic abilities solved the problems, leaving behind bloody noses or unconscious attackers, but they also carried pistols. George recalled, "The revolver we regret, was an indispensable way of success in this country."[11] It is likely that Lees and his boys took away a fair share of Australian gold before they embarked for New Zealand.

While they had the honor of rubbing noses with illustrious Maori chieftains, they had little enthusiasm for the natives' reputation for cannibalism, but the Hanlons' description about 25 years later was perhaps a bit exaggerated:

> The indigenous natives while very amiable in their relations have a disagreeable orientation toward the past. They go to listen to the sermons of a missionary whom they eat very slowly. When they grasp the hand or slap you on the shoulder it is with the intention of knowing if you are fat. They regarded our leaps in the air like one admiring a covey of partridges or a fine butcher's window.[12]

Happy to leave, the gymnasts boarded a sailing ship and spent 37 days getting to the west coast of South America. Starting at Valparaiso, they toured the principal towns of Chile and Peru, working their way up to the Isthmus of Panama. These audiences were enthusiastic and the trip financially successful.

At Aspinwall, Panama, the troupe sailed for Cuba, unaware that tragedy would strike before they arrived.

~

CHAPTER TWO

From 1856
to "Zampillaerostation"

Before leaving panama, Lees was stricken with a dangerous variety of yellow fever, the black vomit. In spite of the best care the boys could summon, he died during the trip to Havana and was buried at sea. Many years later they wryly remarked that it was not only cruel but imprudent for Lees to die in a strange country. Lees had paid little attention to the possibility of dying and left his affairs in relative disorder. The delegated authorities of Cuba settled Lees' estate to suit themselves without taking the boys' advice in the matter. They were left penniless and devastated by the loss of their beloved adopted father.

It was natural that the ten-year global tour produced a special bonding for George, William and Alfred that lasted throughout their lives. In homage to their leader, they adopted the name "Hanlon-Lees," which stayed with them for the rest of their acrobatic career.

After the ship reached Havana, the boys took an engagement with a local circus to get enough money to sail for New York. There they promptly joined the G. F. Bailey Circus and began to tour the country.

It was a hard life. The brothers were now 21, 17 and 14 years of age, but the stunts they could do were not much in America. They had been wonderful in untraveled countries but here there were smarter acrobats with newer tricks. Besides, with Lees gone, their act was like Hamlet with the Dane left out. Forlornly, they wrote to England to ask about their folks, unseen for ten years.

In a western town, while waiting in their dressing room to go on, they suddenly heard a familiar whistle. It was the family signal of the Hanlons. Older brother Tom had crossed the ocean and tracked them by the routes of the show and had come to take them home. They could not have been happier.

Back in Manchester, Tom took charge and turned their house into a gymnasium, where they worked for 18 months to learn new stunts and build a new act.

All six brothers—Tom, George, William, Alfred, Edward and Frederick—formed a company under the name "Hanlon-Lees' Transatlantic Combination," thereby announcing their intention of exploiting two worlds.

They decided to start their second voyage around the world in Paris. George, William and Alfred debuted at the Cirque d'Hiver as "The Three Sons of the Air," and Tom was performing at the Théâtre Porte St. Martin. Their repertoire had been enriched with a number of new tricks, and they no longer held on to the tumbling of Risley. The new act rewarded them after several months with a very attractive proposition for an engagement at St. Petersburg.

On their arrival in Russia, they applied for quarters for their stay, but were turned away because it was supposed they would be very noisy. To overcome this, they paid an exorbitant rent. A part of their work in St. Petersburg was to continue the training of Frederick and Edward, the two youngest members of the group. A gymnasium for practice was built in the house, and their landlord promptly doubled their rent.

The group worked hard on their show, and here they first presented a somersault (*saut périlleux*) which they had invented. William mounted on the shoulders of George, who mounted the shoulders of Thomas, and they remained immobile in that pyramid with their arms folded. All at once, from the top where he was perched, William did a flip and landed on the shoulders of Tom, while George, who was between them, escaped from the pyramid by a somersault and landed on the floor. "This type of trick," said William, "is very difficult. The arms are motionless and to manage without breaking your back requires a great deal of precision."[1]

The show business routine in Russia could be exhausting. During the annual butter fair, long oblong theatres were erected for individual performances. Each show, whatever its kind, was short, but it was repeated many times a day to new audiences. The theatres had many doors and exits and could empty and fill quickly. The act had to be high quality to suit the audience, which often included royalty. On the first day the Hanlons gave nine performances and by the eighth day had worked up to 13 turns. Said William, "I was often too tired to eat on reaching home and it took some will power to muster sufficient energy to go to bed."[2]

On the other hand, the Russian audiences proved friendly and enjoyed the performances immensely. On one occasion the Hanlons, who counted music among their many talents, sent for a set of hand bells and, when they became sufficiently skillful, would give their bearded audiences the Russian national hymn to wild applause. It was less tiring than somersaults.

The men labored all the time inventing novelties and trying them out. One morning after they had moved to the Imperial Circus, William was trying the trapeze. He recalled a terrifying episode:

I called down to George on the stage to take hold of a hanging rope so I could gauge his weight. Hanging from the trapeze by my legs, I pulled George up, hand over hand, a little way and let him down. Some other gymnasts who were looking on said I could not pull him all the way. I said I thought I could and that led to a bet of a breakfast. It was agreed that I could try it at any time I chose within a week.

A night or two later, I suddenly decided to try it during a regular performance and told George, who looked a little queer and asked if I were feeling all right. I said I did.

The pull began. When I had pulled him up within three yards of me, I realized I had done a terrible thing. The pulls became shorter and I dared not attempt to pay out, for I knew I could not control it if I let my muscles relax. It was awful. George saw the situation and was mighty interested. It was life or death for him.

I made a desperate effort, three or four little short pulls and then told George to do something. He did. He made a leap some way with his arms and caught me. I hung on by the legs and he went up over me but I could not get up myself. I was too exhausted. He helped me up and the agony was over. I never made such a bet since.[3]

During a stay in Moscow, a fire broke out in their hotel near the Théâtre Français. The fire started in a library and spread so rapidly they could only watch. The Hanlons and their neighbors, John Henderson and Christophe, two American tightrope walkers who were there with their families, fled to higher floors. The stairs were in flames and collapsing. Ropes were thrown and tied to the windows of neighboring houses and by that aerial route they escaped with the children—"to the acclamation of the crowd which assisted in our dangerous trip, without paying admission," added George.[4]

There is more than one version of the Hanlons' departure from Russia. In their *Mémoires,* the story is one of being lionized and leaving with regrets. The brothers earned a strong following in the country which helped them in official circles. The government made them propositions to stay. They were urged to help found a gymnastics school to which would first be admitted officers of the army and then some elite personnel. The length of their stay was to be about five years, and they would be granted pensions. As attractive as the offers were, the men decided not to accept the proposition. For one thing, the Russian cold bothered them greatly.

The railroads of Russia were not complete, and the brothers felt the winter was a jailer that imprisoned them in the cities nearly two-thirds of the year. But above all they loved France very much and longed to be back, they said. So the brothers went to Paris, say the *Mémoires*.

In later accounts it seems that they became celebrities at the Imperial Circus when William did a double somersault from a trapeze for the first time in Russia. When the performance closed, a new contract at treble the price was waiting for them to sign. When it expired, passports for the group were not available, and they could not leave the country. It happened again at the end of another six months. The British Consul got them out by having them pretend to seek naturalization so that the authorities would forget to enter the prohibition against passports. It worked, and they promptly boarded a ship and fled back to England.[5]

About this time, a new phenomenon burst on the acrobatic scene and captured the Hanlons' attention. A young Frenchman, Jules Leotard, son of a gymnastics instructor, made his debut at the Cirque Napoleon on November 12, 1859. He had originated a special use of the swinging bar known as the flying trapeze. It was an instant success and created a furor. One of the Hanlon boys was sent to check it out.

Later, Leotard came to the Alhambra in London and left two additional marks on history. His name stuck to the tight-fitting costume he wore, and his act inspired the popular song, "The Daring Young Man on the Flying Trapeze."

Back in Manchester in 1859 the brothers made plans to come to America. Unfortunately, William fell 35 feet from a trapeze, broke an arm and could not return to the act for six months.

Despite William's injuries, all six brothers came to America and The Hanlon-Lees Transatlantic Combination continued its tour while William sat on the sidelines. Undoubtedly, the new Leotard technique was percolating in his head.

On January 16, 1860, The Hanlon-Lees appeared with Cook's Circus at Niblo's Gardens in New York City. Their performance was the result of the past several years of practice as a team of six. Tom executed the "Échelle Périlleuse," which consisted of acrobatic stunts performed on a high ladder balanced by one of the brothers. Tom and George appeared in "Parterre," Fred and Edward performed in "Perche," Tom, George and Alfred performed "Pyramid" and Alfred introduced a flying act.

The group moved to Cook's Royal Amphitheatre in Boston and thence back to Niblo's Gardens, where William rejoined the act. By now George and Tom

FIGURE 2. All six Hanlons and their tricks at the Academy of Music, c. 1860. (From the Harvard Theatre Collection, Houghton Library.)

were appearing in "Double Parterre" and Tom, George and William in "Triple Parterre." "Parterre" refers to the orchestra section of the theatre, and these stunts were acrobatics performed in the midst of the audience, forerunners of the sensational flying trapeze act over the auditorium which was yet to come.

The Hanlon-Lees departed on a southern tour and further practice to perfect their version of the flying trapeze introduced by Leotard. When this process was completed to their satisfaction, they headed back to New York to display the re-

FIGURE 3. William Hanlon over the heads of the audience in "Zampillaerostation" at the Academy of Music. (From *Frank Leslie's Illustrated Newspaper*, December 14, 1861.)

sults. As the war between the North and the South had been declared in April 1861, their return north was a prudent decision.

At this point a curious conjunction occurred. In New York, George Fox, the comedian, had formed the G. L. Fox Troupe of American Pantomimists and was playing standard English pantomimes which closely followed the style of the Ravel Family. The Ravel family of pantomimists had come from France and had dominated the bill at Niblo's Gardens for years. Pantomime was beginning to have greater appeal to American audiences.

Fox, along with James Lingard, had some managerial ambitions and rented the Brooklyn Academy of Music to introduce the Hanlon-Lees' new act and also a couple of the Fox pantomimes. The Hanlon-Lees performance was sensational, but Fox's pantos received little attention. Nevertheless, it was an early meeting between two streams of show business activity which were later to be the ingredients of the Hanlons' ultimate career.

On December 12, 1861, William performed for the first time in America the sensational "Zampillaerostation,"[6] a flying trapeze act over the heads of the audience in the auditorium. It was an effort to outdo Leotard.

> From the first tier of boxes which was about 25 feet from the floor of the parquet, a standing place was erected to which was attached an iron ladder. Twenty feet away, in the parquet, stood an iron framework from which hung the first trapeze; 50 feet beyond was a second trapeze, with still another iron framework; 30 feet farther away, the third trapeze was suspended from the proscenium and 18 feet beyond, hanging from the fly gallery, was a wooden frame which was the landing place for the acrobat.
>
> At a given signal, the Hanlon brothers appeared before the immense audience. The acrobats were dressed in plain, black satin tights, with white satin vests and white gloves, the hero of the evening William being specially attired in a fairylike costume of bright silks. After a bow right and left, he took his stand and the brothers advanced to their respective stations. As he arrived at the end of his first swing, he left it and catching the second as it was sent to meet him by his brother, William passed through the air and seized the third swing and finally arrived on the stage. This was a preliminary but the plaudits of the audience shook the building.
>
> Finally for a climax, William went the whole 123 feet like a shot from a cannon and made a double somersault in midair, catching the flying trapeze as he turned and landed on the hanging frame.[7]

Nearly every gymnast in the city was present to witness a great trial of muscular power. The *New York Clipper* of December 21 said that "it was unquestion-

FIGURE 4. William Hanlon stars in "Zampillaerostation" at the Academy of Music. (From the Harvard Theatre Collection, Houghton Library.)

ably the most graceful and perfect acrobatic feat ever attempted. At the conclusion of the feat the applause that greeted the daring performer was terrific and he and his brothers retired in whirlwind of approbation." In many ways this performance was the zenith of the six Hanlon-Lees' careers as world-class acrobats. The *Clipper* commented, "[the act] eclipses that of Leotard or so we have been informed by gentlemen who have witnessed both."

Also appearing at this engagement was "Little Bob," a child acrobat trained by Tom. He was one of several children adopted by the family as apprentices.

With the success at the Academy of Music, the Hanlons apparently felt they had made their point and after a short stay in California, embarked on another world tour. With the Civil War raging, it was a good time to be out of the country. Before they left, Thomas, the eldest brother, was offered the command of a "Corps of Gymnasts" consisting of 5,000 men which the Union government offered to equip. On the advice of their father, they declined because of their many friends on the Confederate side. Nevertheless, the brothers were presented medals inscribed "Gymnasts National of America" by General Sherman on behalf of the people of St. Louis.[8]

Still very young, "The Renowned Hanlons" took delight in performing "difficult, different and dangerous" feats to thrill and shock their spectators. They added a climax to "Zampillaerostation" that was said to be one of the most dangerous acts ever put on the stage. Tom had often used a horizontal ladder hung from the flies over the stage for an acrobatic act called "Leap for Life." In fact, the ladder was set up as the landing place for "Zampillaerostation."

Now, however, they made it a real leap for life. Some distance from one end of the ladder a rope was suspended and held at the bottom by a brother on the stage. The acrobat, having made the trip the length of the auditorium, from trapeze to trapeze, landed on one end of the ladder. Without stopping, he leaped or flew ten feet to the other end of the ladder and finally leaped an incredible 12 feet to the hanging rope. This was a new "Leap for Life."[9] The man holding the rope at the bottom was there primarily to catch the acrobat in case of a miss. There was no net for any of this, and the act no doubt left the audiences limp.

In the next three years the Hanlons' travels included New Granada, Bolivia, Chile, England, Ireland, Scotland, Wales, France, Germany, Spain, Portugal and returning through Brazil to the United States in 1865.

Young and fearless, the brothers knew that daredevil stunts performed out of doors were sure-fire material for spreading the Hanlon name and reputation. In Baltimore, at the top of the highest monument in the city, William held Alfred by the ankles as he dangled over the edge. People passing were horrified to see a man apparently on the point of falling to earth and called the police. William deftly pulled Alfred back, but they were met on the stairs by a policeman who booked them for "attempted suicide." For several hours they were detained for their recklessness on top of the monument. Newspapers, of course, carried the story.

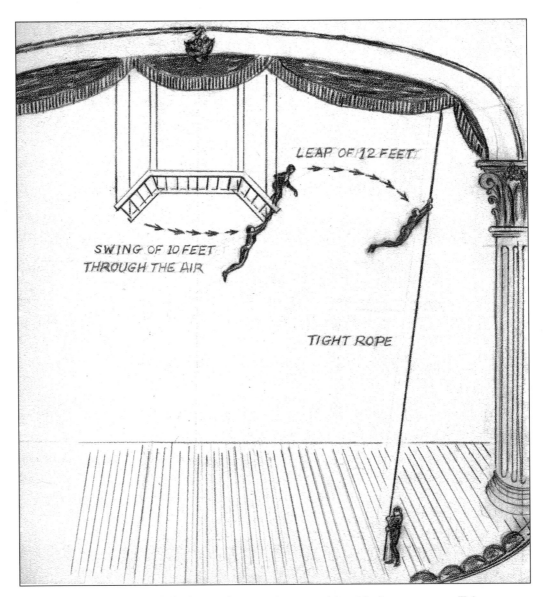

FIGURE 5. "Leap for Life," after a diagram in an unidentified newspaper, February 24, 1924.

Inevitably there were falls during rehearsal or performance. The brothers sometimes debated whether a person could keep a clear head during a fall. Edward maintained it was possible. At the New Orleans Academy, while performing a complicated ladder feat, he was ready to jump and was waiting for a brother to cry "Go" when he heard a woman say "Oh" and mistook the cry for his brother's. He jumped but there was no one to catch him. "As I passed a balcony," reported Edward, "I noted a woman with a red fan and heard her scream." He landed in a soldier's lap.

"I wasn't hurt and neither was the soldier but he was white as a sheet. My legs broke the backs of two chairs," said Edward. "I proved that one does think while passing through space." He told his brothers about the lady he had noted in the balcony with her red fan.

"You're right," they reported. "That woman fainted and had to be taken from the theatre just after you heard her scream."[10]

With the Civil War over, the way seemed clear for further triumphs before American audiences. Fate, however, took a hand, and another tragedy was to shape the Hanlons' future career.

CHAPTER THREE

~

1865–1869: Tragedy and a Change of Course

1865 WAS A FATEFUL YEAR for the six brothers. Two events changed their lives forever.

At a Chicago engagement, they met Henri Agoust, a French juggler and all-around showman. He had experience in ballet, fencing, magic and, most importantly, in pantomime. He saw that the Hanlons were not above mixing a little comedy with their daredevil acrobatics and introduced them to the pantomime traditions of Debureau and the fantasy plays of the Theatre of Funambules. Agoust persuaded the Hanlons to begin rehearsing two of Debureau's pantomimes, *Harlequin Statue* and *Harlequin Skeleton*. It was a seed that took a while to blossom fully, but when it did, it made pantomime history.

The other stroke of fate that followed quickly was the tragic accident which befell Thomas at Pike's Opera House in Cincinnati on August 14, 1865. Accounts differ, but while performing "Échelle Périlleuse" (Dangerous Ladder) or "Leap for Life," Thomas fell, hitting his head on one of the gas jets in the footlights. His injuries were very severe and the permanent pain excruciating. He could work only in fits and starts until his bizarre suicide less than three years later.[1]

The effect of Tom's accident on the team was profound. There had been a number of falls previously; Tom had had two, but none so serious. The Hanlon families were distressed, and their parents exacted promises that the acrobats find safer employment. One result was the splitting apart of the group and an obvious casting about for new specialties. There was a determined effort to develop greater skill at pantomime.

One experiment which illustrates the Hanlon fondness for all sorts of spectacles was their purchase of "The Oracle of the Sphinx." At the Egyptian Hall in London, Colonel Stodare had introduced a new illusion. He carried out a small box, placed it on an undraped table and opened the front. Inside was a disembod-

20

ied head. At his command, the "Sphinx" opened his eyes, smiled and responded to questions from the audience.

When the Hanlons in New York heard of it, they instructed William, who was temporarily abroad, to buy the secret of the Sphinx. The price was 5,000 francs. This was expensive, but the group hoped to make a deal with P. T. Barnum and arranged a demonstration for him.

When he saw it, Barnum appeared satisfied with the effect, which he attributed to a mechanical head and a speaking tube. He was mistaken. Actually it was an optical trick invented and built by Thomas Tobin in England. Two mirrors met at a 45-degree angle under the three-legged table, reflected the side curtains and created the illusion that one had a clear view to the back curtain. The mirrors concealed the body of the Sphinx.

In the middle of the Hanlons' negotiations with Barnum, the impresario recalled correspondence with his agents in England and a letter announcing the purchase of a Sphinx effect similar to what he had just seen. The Hanlons withdrew gracefully and agreed with the great showman that they would only present the attraction in cities outside New York.

The Sphinx was expected to be a great success, but it didn't materialize. The care the Hanlons took to hide the secret of the spectacle aroused the curiosity of their employees. One of their mechanics, at considerable peril, climbed on the roof of the theatre, broke a hole and descended into the flies. He managed to observe the preparation. The secret was immediately exposed. The Hanlons concluded that their employees would not be happy promoting or exhibiting anything which required hiding the secret from them. George, who was always deeply religious, attached a moral to the incident: "Religious rites should not have secrets from priests who perform them."[2]

The Hanlons continued to explore new roles and appeared on a variety bill at the Continental Theatre early in 1866. This show began with a romantic playlet and ended with Sylvester's Enchanted Fountains, a stage effect imported from England that produced "dancing waters and a shower of gold and gems." The vehicle for this machine was a fairy play which introduced Apollo, the God of Music, and the Crystal Grotto of the Naiades. Fred was in the cast as an attendant goblin. The Hanlons' penchant for elaborately coined titles for their acts surfaced again when Alfred was listed on the bill in "Aeropateticism" and the Hanlon Brothers offered "Anabathron!"—acrobatics by another name.

Bookings were hard to come by, and the brothers felt they had to split up. Various arrangements were tried. George, William and Alfred had a natural affinity and for a time formed the Hanlon and Zanfretta Combination under the

FIGURE 6. Frederick, Thomas and Edward (*left to right*) in their "European Combination." (From the Harvard Theatre Collection, Houghton Library.)

management of Morris Simmonds to tour west and south. Alex and Josie Zanfretta and M. Chenat were in the company.

Edward and Frederick, the younger brothers, together with Thomas, who was struggling to recover and return, formed another combination. Playbills show that this company included the Siegrist Family, Señorita Stella, tightrope; Master George, child wonder of trapeze; Annetta Galletti, danseuse; the Caron Family of French pantomime; G. W. Smith, ballet master; Charles Collins' infant prodigies, Tom, Dick and Harry, 3, 4 and 6 years old. This group was managed by Dr. Charles Brown.

Each group continued to put together various entertainment offerings. Early in 1868, George, William and Alfred were presenting The Great Hanlon Transatlantic Combination for several weeks at the Theatre Comique in New York. An early program line-up consisted of the following, with many of the acts imported from England or the Continent:

Mlle. Gertrude and her Enchanting Quadrupeds (dogs)
The Three Flying Men of the Air (George, William and Alfred)
Revels of Oberon on Revolving Orbs (Jean, Victor and Albert)
Harry Gurr, Mysterious Amphibious Mortal (a champion English swimmer
    who could eat, drink and smoke a cigar under water)
Les Deux Chapeaux (hat juggling by William and Alfred)
Triple Horizontal Bars (Arthur, Albert, Jean and Victor)
Les Grostêtes (giant grotesque heads)
Hanlon's Grand Miniature Circus and the Lilliputian Steeple Chase (trick
    ponies)

As the bill changed, other acts were introduced:

Le Petit Ethardo (perilous ascent on the illuminated mountain)[3]
Carleton
Pantomimes (Hanlons in "The Perpetual Torment" and the "Village Torment")

It was a time when one or another of the brothers was making a trip to England or France hoping to find novelty to exploit. One of the things which attracted William was the new invention in England and France known as a velocipede. This was a two-wheel riding device, somewhat like our bicycle but with pedals on cranks on the front wheel. Early spokes were wood and tires were iron. Velocipedes took considerable skill to operate. William promptly incorporated them into a sketch and premiered them as a stage prop in England. He brought some back to America.

FIGURE 7. Playbill misidentifying Frederick, Thomas and Edward (*left to right*), who perform with their pupils, Julien, François and Victor, and a bill of variety acts. (From the Harvard Theatre Collection, Houghton Library.)

BOSTON THEATRE.

J. B. BOOTH, - - - - - - - - - - - - - LESSEE AND MANAGER

Wednesday, October 23, and Every Night,

Also Saturday Afternoon, at 2 1-2 O'clock,

'The Hanlon Brothers'

(George, William, and Alfred.)

Grand Transatlantic Combination of Male & Female Continental Artists

Their First Appearance in America.

The performance on WEDNESDAY and THURSDAY EVENINGS will commence with the amusing Farce of

A CONJUGAL LESSON!

Mr. Simon Lullaby . . . . Mr. C. R. Thorne, Jr
Mrs. Letitia Lullaby, (her first appearance here) . . . . Miss Julia Gaylord

SELECTIONS BY - - - - - - - - THE ORCHESTRA

Centrifugal Tourniquets . . . . . . **William and Alfred**

This great Act of Entortilation, the most difficult in the whole range of the Gymnasia, and certainly the most arduous ever achieved by the Brothers, is the sole and joint invention of William and Alfred, and by them respectfully and cordially recommended as a new field for Professors and the Amateur Gymnasts of the United States. It will be found a valuable acquisition to the Gymnasium.

PYRAMIDE CRYSTALE . . . . **GEORGE HANLON**

M'LLE GERTUDE AND HER TROUPE OF ELFIN FRENCH POODLES!
In a series of novel and amusing ecentricities.

L'ECHELLE PENDANT . . . . **LE PETITE ETHARDO**

Revels of Oberon on Revolving Orbs . . . . Ethardo, Albert, Jean and Victor
Concluding with
THE SPIRAL ASCENSION, by . . . . **ETHARDO**

HARRY GURR, THE CHAMPION SWIMMER

In his marvellous Aquatic Evolutions, in an immense body of **Real Water**, wherein he will be seen to EAT, DRINK, SMOKE, and perform the most astonishing and scarcely credible feats, equally as difficult as if immersed in the BED OF THE OCEAN.
The London Press have pronounced Mr. GURR a lineal descendant of NEPTUNE and AMPHITRITE. The Lancashire worthies, in their editorials, style him a SUBMARINE MONSTER, and the Cornish Press, a TRITON, or Amphibious Nonentity.

Les Deux Chapeaux - - - - - - - **William and Alfred**
Tripple Horizontal Bars - - - - - Ethardo, Albert, Jean and Victor

To conclude with Hanlon's

GRAND MINIATURE CIRCUS!

Introducing the **Highly trained Steed "DIANA"** and the **Celebrated Quadruped Artist "JUPITER,"** (the only Dog in the World that has been taught to Ride, Vault, Leap Balloons, &c., &c., rivalling the most Accomplished Equestrians of the Day,) terminating with the Exciting, Marvellous, Mirth-Provoking Act, by the whole of the Canine Fraternity, entitled the

LILLIPUTIAN STEEPLE CHASE!

☞ NOTICE.—Opera Glasses of superior quality can be hired at the stand in the Lobby of the Theatre.

This establishment has recently been provided by the American Fire Extinguisher Co. with three of their celebrated Fire Annihilators.

PRICES OF ADMISSION:

Balcony Chairs	$1.00	Dress Circle	50 Cents
Parquet	75 Cents	Family Circle	30 Cents
Orchestra Chairs	$1.00	Private Boxes	Accoding to Location

Box Office open daily from 8 1-2 A. M., to 10 P. M. Seats Secured Six Days in advance.
Doors open at 7 . . . . Overture commences at 7 1-2.

FIGURE 8. George, William and Alfred tour with their "Grand Transatlantic Combination" of gymnastic and specialty acts, 1867–68. (From the Harvard Theatre Collection, Houghton Library.)

Very shortly, when the show moved to Boston, where the Hanlons were to appear as a feature act in a minstrel show, Harry McGlennan, business manager of Selwyn's Theatre, induced them to ride their velocipedes on Boston Common as a publicity stunt. This created a furor, and thousands of people turned out to see the phenomenon. It was the beginning of the craze for velocipedes in America. As Edward put it, "The idea of flying through the air like a witch on a broomstick seemed to have great fascination."[4] Fred Hanlon was the best rider among the acrobats and for a number of years held first honors for speed and agility.

~   ~

Meanwhile, Tom had grown worse and had been placed in an asylum in Harrisburg, Pa. One night when the intense pain awakened him, he got up and, being alone in the room, climbed atop a bureau and forced himself to dive headlong into a cast iron heating pipe which crossed the room. The asylum attendants heard dull thuds repeated at regular intervals but didn't understand the cause. They counted 17. When they went to Thomas' room to investigate, a little late, they found him lying on the floor, his head entirely shattered. He died April 5, 1868.[5]

~   ~

In July 1868 a United States patent was awarded to the five living brothers. It was for a velocipede with both wheels of the same size. (See Appendix B.) The Hanlons made arrangements with a carriage manufacturer named Calvin Witty to have bicycles manufactured, and opened Velocipede Hall at 786–788 Broadway for the sale and exhibition of these new machines. For a time they were the best-selling models in the country and the Hanlons were swamped with orders. Witty, however, wouldn't speed up manufacture. Hundreds of letters, some including money, arrived, begging the Hanlons to send anything that looked like a bicycle but the demands could not be met. The venture was short-lived.[6]

More successfully, the Hanlons opened a velocipede school at Broadway and Ninth Street to teach bicycle riding. Colonel John Jacob Astor attended the school, as did Charles Dana, editor of the *Sun*, and his son, Paul Dana. A second patent for velocipede improvements was issued February 9, 1869, to William with his brothers as assignors.

Because the Hanlons frequently used the velocipedes in their act, it was a powerful promotion that expanded the market for manufacturers who followed behind them.

Troublesome infringements of their patents and the call of show business soon led them to abandon the bicycle as a business. The patents were sold to Colonel Albert Pope. William said, "The last time I saw one of our 'improved velocipedes' was witnessing George L. Fox, the famous clown in *Humpty-Dumpty*, go to heaven on it in a transformation scene at the Olympic Theater, New York."[7]

For a time, the bicycle had proved to be a popular attraction, and in later years the brothers delighted in telling a story of show business one-upmanship.

David Bidwell of the New Orleans Academy of Music had refused to meet the Hanlons' demand for a higher fee and said he would fight them if they tried to go to another theatre. The Hanlons, unafraid, went to Ben De Bar of St. Louis, who owned the St. Charles Theatre in New Orleans, and signed for a date. As Edward tells it in a newspaper interview,

> We had a manager, Ned Kendall, a splendid fellow but every now and then would drink too much. We explained our plan and sent him off to New Orleans with the order to stay sober and the promise that if it worked, he could drown himself in liquor. Kendall gave a little supper for all the billposters and when it was over he had signed contracts for all the bill-board space in the city. Then he covered every inch of it with posters announcing the Hanlon Brothers would appear at the St. Charles Theatre. Bidwell was furious and sent for bill posters to paste something, anything over our printing but the men had signed our contracts. They would not comply.
>
> We knew Bidwell was a good fighter. His blood was up and would do something unexpected to offset us. For the occasion he brought in a circus he owned then performing in Texas.[8] It cost an immense sum of money. On opening day the circus procession was ready to start with the head just opposite the St. Charles Theatre, the band wagon, elephants, camels and chariots all waiting. The command was given for the parade to start and instantly my brothers, dressed as jockeys, dashed out on their wheels and rode off before the first animal was in motion. The crowd was jammed in the street but it parted and then followed the newfangled contraptions, leaving the circus procession to parade by itself. The bicycle had made its first appearance in New Orleans.
>
> We rode them on the stage that night and on the street. Wherever we appeared we were followed by curious crowds. Bidwell had us arrested for driving carriages on the sidewalk but the mayor released us when he saw the machines.
>
> We did an immense business and that was the last and only fight we had with Bidwell. Actually he liked pluck and afterwards when we came back we played his theatre.[9]

Even before this, the brothers were tired of being separated and competing for pick-up variety engagements. For October 31, 1868, the Holliday Theatre announced: "Last Night / Re-union and Farewell Tour of the Hanlon Brothers! George, William, Alfred, Edward and Frederick with their adopted pupils, Julien, François and Victor!" This engagement also promised "The Famous Young Russian Athlete, PFAU on the flying trapeze." A line at the bottom of the broadside offered: "Hanlon patented velocipede for sale at 638 Broadway."

A year later, in November 1869, the five brothers were still bidding farewell at Tammany Hall, New York City, "their first appearance in four years in a theater." It was a hybrid act that saw their aerial acrobatics greatly diminished. The "Great Act" featured "Little Bob." As described by a reviewer:

> Horizontal bars which seem about two feet apart are swung parallel with the footlights at a height of about thirty feet above them. At the two ends of these bars, and also about thirty feet from each other, Alfred and Frederick Hanlon station themselves, hanging head down from [a trapeze] . . . they swing back and forth, sustaining themselves by the calf of the leg. One of the brothers seizes a child, "little Bob" who looks about eight years of age. The gymnast . . . flies back and forth . . . like a pendulum holding the child now by the hands now by the legs. Suddenly he hurls the child through the intervening space and the little fellow is safely caught by the other brother. . . . This is repeated with variations but always with the most perfect precision and elegance. In one instance the child turns a complete somersault. . . .[10]

For the first time, Little Bob and the apprentices worked with a safety net, a Hanlon invention. Throughout their career, the original Hanlon brothers had never had the protection of a net. They presented the idea to the New York Fire Department as a possible lifesaving device, and the Department made it practical by substituting canvas in a ring for the Hanlons' rope net.

Other acts named on the Tammany Hall bill were:

Lilliputian Gladiators in Midair (Julian and Victor Hanlon)
"À pas Africaine" (Julian, Victor and Little Bob)
Pantomimes: "Le Chapeau Magique" (with George and Edward Hanlon) and
    "The Village Torment" (with the original Hanlons)

In many ways this engagement marked the passing of an era. The five brothers were together again but entering a totally different phase. In a couple of months they went to Europe and were not to return to the United States for more than ten years.

One thing frequently mentioned by reviewers was the brothers' great linguistic ability and command of many foreign languages. Small wonder in light of their constant world travel, but a curious accomplishment for men who later earned great fame as pantomimists!

On the eve of their departure, William wrote to C. Allston Brown of the *New York Clipper*, asking for mention that the brothers and Little Bob had succeeded in doing a Double Backward Somersault from hands to hands in mid-air. The men were stationed 20 feet apart. "This feat was performed for the first time by any artists by Alfred and Frederick Hanlon and Little Bob at the Front Street Theatre, Baltimore, January 19, 1870."[11]

CHAPTER FOUR

Pantomime from 1870

ENGLAND AND THE CONTINENT nurtured a long tradition in pantomime that went through many changes from its early beginnings in Italian commedia dell'arte. *The Oxford Companion to the Theatre* cites seven varieties of pantomime, but it is certain that the divisions have been by no means clear cut. As more formal conventions involving stock characters such as Pierrot, Columbine and Harlequin became less popular, pantomime was often whatever the pantomime producer threw into the theatrical pot. A bit of harlequinade, a clown, some trick scenery, acrobatics and a transformation, all presented more or less in dumb show, was a common recipe.

In America, early pantomimes had a mixed reception. Form and talent were largely imported from abroad, but ritualized stories and dumb show were not immediately accepted by American audiences, who favored melodrama and farce.

However, the Ravel family of pantomimists came from France in the early 19th century to Park Theatre in New York and dominated the bill at Niblo's Gardens for years. Their skilled acrobatics, comedy, dance and mechanical stage tricks were popular with metropolitan audiences. Eventually they became a strong influence on American theatre. An old-time showman recalled a particular piece of Ravel trickwork:

> Garibaldi Ravel, father of all the Ravels, was crushed as flat as a pancake by a thing looking like a big millstone that three or four men rolled out on the stage. It accidently tipped over and Garibaldi was caught under it. When the huge grindstone was lifted up with the help of more men who were called in, Garibaldi looked like a great cut-out of a paper man. A lounge was procured and the paper man was laid on it. Then one of the Ravels rushed out, procured a pair of bellows and commenced to blow it up. The figure gradually assumed its normal shape. Instantly Garibaldi jumped from the lounge a newly made man and took his customary bow.[1]

The Ravels were associated with the Zanfrettas, the Martinettis, the Marzettis and many other pantomime artists and acrobats from Europe. By 1862, the Ravel family was featuring "Young America," a handsome and daring youngster in a flying trapeze act. His actual name was John H. Haslam. Many years later he joined the Hanlons as a pantomimist and stage manager with the *Fantasma* and *Superba* shows.

In the late 1860s, George Fox, a famous American comedian, starred in *Humpty-Dumpty,* a show that was staged in the Ravel style. Fox as a clown gave his pantomime a more distinctly American flavor. The show was hugely successful and was the first panto to be presented as a full evening's entertainment. Pantomime gained popularity. Many producers began imitations.

None of this was lost on the Hanlons. As we have seen, they had begun to work with the Zanfrettas and Siegrists and were already appearing in their own interpretations of French pantomimes.

Agoust, who had first persuaded the Hanlon-Lees to perform a pantomime in 1865, continued his association with the Hanlons and, after the death of Thomas, tended to fill that vacancy. When the group returned to France in 1870, their first engagement was with Frederick Strange, an English director. He was the man who had brought Leotard to the Alhambra in London and now had come to Paris to mount a splendid English ballet pantomime, *Fiamma.* It was an adventure story which incorporated clowns, gymnasts, tricks and machines. Agoust and the brothers filled in with acrobatics. Unfortunately, the Franco-Prussian War had begun, and when the Empire fell, the show folded.

The Hanlons saw that it was necessary to leave Paris but Agoust refused to go, left the troupe and enlisted in the Paris National Guard during the siege of the city. The brothers retired to the provinces to wait out the war.

Actually hostilities were short-lived. *Les Frères Hanlon-Lees* were back in town at the already famous Folies Bergère in little more than six months. Their show, booked by Leon Sari in November 1872, as shown in the accompanying illustration, included the following:

Le Dortoit (acrobatics on flying rings and trapeze performed while "asleep")
Échelle Perilleuse (comedy acrobatics on the ladder)
La Salle à Manger (a dignified dinner scene in which the acrobats upset all laws
    of politeness)
Frater de Village (pantomime)
Le Saut Perilleux (trapeze somersaults by Little Bob)
Chapeaux Magiques (juggling sketch with hats)

FIGURE 9. The Hanlon-Lees headline with comedy acrobatics and pantomimes at Folies Bergère, Paris. (From *La Vie Parisienne*, November 9, 1872, in the Boston Public Library, Rare Books Department.)

FIGURE 10. The "Great Act" with Little Bob was a Hanlon-Lees feature at the Folies Bergère. (From *L'Univers Illustré,* November 16, 1872, in the Boston Public Library, Rare Books Department.)

The troupe had a small repertoire of shorter, traditional sketches they had been performing in America. These first pantomimes were simple plots that the brothers embroidered with their unique knock-about gymnastics. "Frater de Village" (The Village Barber) is a good example:

The village barber is in love with a beautiful girl (Columbine) whose barbarous parents want her to marry a rich man. The lover loses his head and will stop at nothing to win her. The family is dining peacefully when the storm suddenly breaks. The barber (Pierrot) appears with wild hair and white powdered face, armed with a foaming wash tub and a giant razor. He asks himself, "How can these dining people refuse me their daughter? I will shave them!"

He inadvertently whacks the heads off several persons in the way but later carefully repairs the damage using sealing wafers. Columbine's parents remain stubborn so he tries to soften them by soaking them in the wash tub. They will not be softened and a fight breaks out in which Columbine and her mother get their share of the slaps and kicks. The father finally concedes.[2]

The bare bones of "Frater de Village" may seem mindless but the buffoonery and gymnastics of the Hanlons made it a wild success.

Thomas Walton commented: "For over a century English pantomimists had been celebrated in France for their eccentricity, their awe-inspiring rough and tumble. The Hanlon-Lees startled even English audiences. . . . Violence was a characteristic of their work from the very beginning; it was one of their greatest attractions in the eyes of Parisians when in 1872, Leon Sari let them loose on the stage of . . . Folies Bergère."[3]

As daredevil aerial acrobatics faded, the same skills and energy were poured into longer pantomimes. Every day the five brothers met at the theatre at one o'clock to brainstorm for their next opus. William was a leader in arranging scenarios and Alfred the music. They claimed never to write a script but trusted to memory. Out of this collaboration came a series of bizarre but highly successful pantomimes having little to do with traditional pantomime forms.

Among the earliest were "Pierrot Menuisier" (Coffin-maker), "Singes et Baigneuses" (Monkeys and Bathers), "Les Quatre Pipelettes" (The Four Lady Porters) and "Pierrot Terrible."

In these works the brothers raised their eccentricity to high art and soon became the rage of Paris. In "Pierrot Menuisier," Pierrot sells upholstered coffins to people. When he kills a man for declining to purchase, he is haunted by the man's ghost wearing the coffin he had tried to sell him. As gendarmes approach, Pierrot fires a gun and hits a pregnant cat producing a hailstorm of kittens falling on the stage.

The action in "Pierrot Terrible," as seen in a condensed translation from *Les Mémoires,* was typical:

The stage is a public square. On the left is a bakery complete with tubs, baskets, paddles and kneading boards; on the right a butcher shop with chains, hooks, saws and cleavers. In the center is a fashionable tailor shop.

The sign on the tailor shop attracts a passing dandy. The tailor is away but two Pierrots obsequiously do the honors for the shop. They charm the prospect—Please be seated!—and circle around him like lions ready to devour him. Their first act is to undress him from head to toe. "Bon Dieu! M. Leandre, what rags you are wearing! What a hat, what a coat, what a vest! Let us throw this trash into the gutter."

"But you have left me nude!" said Leandre, his modesty shocked. "It's nothing" the Pierrots reassure him with a flurry of thumps, fillips, slaps and blows.

They begin to take the measurements of their client who has a simple, idiotic expression. They spare nothing. They line him up, they survey him. They evaluate him with cord, with a sextant, with a yard stick. They measure him for a cane, a dagger and a breast pin—not without strangling him, turning him upside down, mauling him and planting surveying stakes in his shoulders. He must suffer to be handsome and when it is done he becomes superb.

"Here is Leandre as good as new, all ready to steal the hearts of willing ladies. Never have we seen a man so well turned out."

The Pierrots are enchanted with their work. "It is important to sign the masterpiece we have created." They find a large seal and stick it on the rear end of their client, and so it can be seen without difficulty, they cut off the tails of Leandre's coat.

All this work makes the Pierrots hungry. They decide to lunch and enter the butcher shop next door but they are unwilling to buy sheep's heads which sneeze and wink their eyes. The calves lick their hands and display tongues several feet long. The butcher is an expansive man who waves his knives around so hard that he carves his customers as readily as he does his merchandise. This irritates the Pierrots and they bury him under his legs of mutton and beefsteaks and wreck the shop. "That'll teach him."

The bakery has a better appearance. The friendly owner has them admire his establishment and his roaring ovens. A little boy comes in to buy a roll and is put in the oven without thinking. It is pure inadvertence—don't pay any attention.

Truly, here are fine cookies. The Pierrots' mouths water. They select a pastry but the moment they go to bite, the cakes move. The cakes have little feet and escape when they go to eat them. The cakes march in protest. The chocolate hornets are really hornets and the spice bricks are truly paving bricks.

A new flood of slaps, blows from fists and feet erupt. The scuffle goes on inside and outside the ovens. Ten o'clock strikes. Time to go to bed.

All the shops are closed. The Pierrots can't sleep because a bored statue yawns and stretches. They invite the statue to supper but it refuses. The Pierrots are displeased. They drag the statue off the pedestal, put its neck in a door and signal the police to arrest this loitering drunk. Police take the statue to the station. The statue protests and is certain the mayor will be unhappy.

The Pierrots decide to sleep under the stars but the ground is hard and will make them hunchbacked. The two demand to know why they can't sleep comfortably in the neighboring house where there are probably persons who do not occupy their entire bed. They have only to squeeze to make a small place. So they approach the house of a banker with the resolve to steal if they are accorded hospitality. They enter after picking the lock.

The banker sleeps like a rogue with a clear conscience. He had forgotten to lock his strong box which is stuffed with riches. The sweet man! He has the indelicacy to stir in his sleep. Pierrot seizes a sack, another and another. The work charms him so much he can't stop. He loads himself like a donkey. He staggers under the burden. The floor boards crack under his feet. Another sack, the last. . . . Bang! Pierrot and the sacks tumble to the ground. The banker wakes up. They cry, they scream, they battle. It's an indescribable melee. In the middle of this one notices Harlequin.

Harlequin doesn't appear for nothing. He pays more than a little attention to the wife of the banker, but Columbine keeps her distance. He strolls around the beauty with a guilty air and at that moment Pierrot re-enters, fatigued. Lord is he fatigued! [In traditional pantomime, Harlequin was often the *deus ex machina* who controlled people and caused magic effects.]

Pierrot realizes the banker's bed is free. Without a care he lies down grandly, intending to sleep like a mouse. He is thrilled with the prospect but as he slides under the covers he discovers that the bed is occupied by a pretty woman.

A burglar, but virtuous, Pierrot recoils in shock. The white shoulders of Madame Columbine scandalize him. He withdraws with modesty but not without remarking that young women sleep a lot. He comports himself like a gentleman and seeing that he respects Columbine it is only fair that he study her a little.

Pierrot pulls back the quilt with infinite care and Columbine, who is happily sleeping in a short petticoat, is revealed to his delighted eyes like a vision. Pierrot in transport, goes to present his respects to the lady but she disappears into the mattress. [The trick is the work of Harlequin, who appears at this moment, but also of stage mechanics. The bed has a trap.]

Pierrot shakes off his romantic ideas and throws himself into bed. This time nothing emerges from the mattress, but as an additional precaution, he carefully shuts all the doors.

Sweet sleep. It is the hour when rats emerge from their holes and go promenading on the quilts of unsuspecting sleepers. Pierrot awakens to find himself nose to nose with horrible vermin. They are enormous. They pretend to scatter but return, arrogant, noisy and swarming, until Pierrot wages such a battle that they eventually give way and disappear.

One can't sleep after so much emotion. Pierrot decides to read. Unfortunately, the banker uses special candles subject to sudden flaming. Pierrot tries to make the candle stand still but the situation suddenly unravels. The candles set fire to the house.

Then begins the final uproar of the pantomime. The hubbub with firemen, policemen, clowns, villagers, dancers, and maids in petticoats is fantastique. One of the maids is in grave danger. Pierrot is not without sympathy. The danger to the old woman brings him to tears. He leaps upon her, lifts her, spins her around, drags her from the flames and sends her plunging, head first into the big bass drum in the orchestra. That generous act transfigures him and he mounts to the sky, resplendent in a stream of sparks.

It is well to remember that Pierrot's lines represented in this description as quotations were actually conveyed to the audience in pantomime. The Hanlons had mastered the art of "speaking" by means of eloquent facial expressions and body language. One has to recall silent movies without captions to capture a feeling for this performance. It is also apparent that the frenzy and violence of their sketches lived on in the film work of Buster Keaton, the Marx Brothers and the Three Stooges.

With these successes their fame was ensured, and the Hanlon-Lees went on an extended European tour, appearing in Spain, Italy, Germany and St. Petersburg.

While touring in 1876, the brothers again met their old friend Agoust at the Walhalla in Berlin. He was out of the army and back in the theatre. At the time they were trying to stage a new pantomime, *Do Mi Sol Do*. The idea came from a sketch in a blackface minstrel show which got its humor from the rehearsal of an amateur orchestra. The Hanlons thought they could add something but they lacked a competent conductor. Agoust took the part.

The *Do Mi Sol Do* scene was the sort that the Hanlons reveled in—choreographed mayhem. The musicians slowly begin to sabotage the orchestra rehearsal and the conductor in a thousand ways. The melee mounts in crescendo but throughout, the maestro remains above the fray, impassive, preoccupied with his vision of a great masterpiece. Here are a few incidents:

> When the scene opens the musicians face one another with bows in hand and deliver mutual short raps on the head like an orchestra leader beginning an overture. The symphony bursts like a clap of thunder. There is a chirping of quavers, thumps, slaps to the face, stomping of feet, and banging to wake the dead. In unison they sound an A and stop. They bow, brush themselves off and those who have survived turn the page of music and lift their arms.
>
> The maestro directs the symphony, oblivious to the results. All the scraping, blowing and rebellious stomping respond to his gestures. His supremacy is total; his grandeur overwhelms them. The mad musicians tear off the tails of his coat. The maestro sways like a stalk of wheat in the breeze; he is sweet, masterful and indescribable. His orchestra which he holds in his palm is full of exquisite shadings. There are pianissimos where not intended and crescendos where the last note is an explosion.
>
> A talented violinist begins a lovely solo but the violin is loaded and when the audience least expects it, the violin goes off and hurts his hand. He stops and listens. The note is too low. He tries again and the violin fires even louder. The maestro doesn't notice. It is futile to shatter furniture on his head. He is calm, immutable, smiling, working on the grand composition in his head. The free-for-all goes on. Aerial trains pass by spewing rockets on the actors' dishevelled wigs. The musicians have lost their music. They finally tie up their leader and drag him out by the feet.[4]

Do Mi Sol Do met with extraordinary success at the Folies Bergère. The Hanlon-Lees had been engaged for a month at a salary of 360 pounds, but after the first evening they signed an agreement for 600 pounds per month and played the pantomime for 13 months running. From this point on, the Hanlon-Lees worked hard on developing new pantomimes that showed off their unrivaled acrobatic skills and satisfied the French audiences' taste for the macabre. "We envisioned a series of works where fantasy, agility and true realism play an equal part," said George.

Les Cascades du Diable (Fits of the Devil), also with Agoust, followed *Do Mi Sol Do*. As the curtain rises in Hell, Satan releases some damned souls to visit a party on earth. The clowns play at ninepins with coconuts, and wrestle with an elephant. One of the Pierrots is a doctor who tries to vaccinate a nursery full of howling babies. Another finds an immense bottle of milk and bibs. A maze of long tubes is attached to the bottle and placed in the mouths of the kids, who quit crying and drain the bottle.

The final scene is a masterpiece of trickwork. Pierrot is up a ladder lighting a street lamp when the ladder disappears. (A French reviewer remarked that Pierrot's frantic acrobatic attempts to reach the lamp were impossible to describe.) Finally, a house collapses on itself. Harlequin and Columbine are revealed dancing on the ruins. Satan swings his pitchfork and blesses his subjects in a superb apotheosis. All the damned return to the fires except one Countess, who exits by ascending to Paradise.[5]

One day while the Hanlon-Lees were rehearsing at the Folies, M. Jules Coquelin, of the Comédie Français, appeared with a manuscript under his arm—an inspiration, he said, of the night before. He was very urgent that the Hanlons should play it as a pantomime. He called it "Le Dentiste." The brothers played it, and it created a sensation.

Shortly after, Henri de Villemosant, editor of *Figaro,* wrote the Hanlons requesting them to contribute to an improvised entertainment which he was arranging in honor of the Grand Dukes Constantine and Alexis of Russia. The Hanlons discovered that the theatre and the office of *Figaro* were very small indeed. They had nothing in their repertoire that would fit. Not wanting to refuse, they invented something for the occasion, a sketch called "The Duel." The sketch ends with a *deus ex machina* bull striking off Pierrot's head. Pierrot, "gushing like a rocket," falls into the arms of Henry IV and Napoleon!

Captive ballooning was fashionable in Paris at the time, made more so by the repeated ascensions of Sarah Bernhardt. The Hanlons tried it out a number of times with thought of some daring feat, but that never materialized. Venturing further, two brothers tried free ballooning. One Saturday afternoon two balloons ascended from the gas factory at Villette. The *Ville de Lyon,* piloted by M. Louis Godard, bore George Hanlon and some Italian royalty aloft. At the same time, *Le Pilote,* piloted by M. Duruof, carried Alfred.

Duruof's flight took more than four hours but due to the variable winds, landed only 15 kilometers from the point of departure. Godard's passengers reported it to be an "indescribable spectacle" and marveled over the distant mountain peaks, the iridescent clouds and what appeared to be frozen lakes.[6]

At some point in this period, the Hanlons appeared in a fantastic play involving a shipwreck. It was remarkable as a tour de force in scenic trickwork. Scenes of boats sailing on the ocean had long been a tradition in French theatre, and the Hanlons added their inimitable gymnastics to the genre. Georges Moynet describes the Hanlons' scenario for an ill-fated sea voyage.[7]

When the curtain rises, the audience sees a shipping dock with buildings receding in the distance and masts of boats tied up alongside. A packetboat which takes up a good part of the stage setting is moored alongside the wharf. Various scenes unfold as travelers mount the gangway to the rear deck of the ship.

The captain and the helmsman climb the gangway. A bell and whistle give a signal to depart. The funnel belches smoke and the ship gets underway. The actors remaining on the dock wave with cries of "adieu" as the audience watches them disappear. [The ship remains in place and the shoreline moves out of

FIGURE 11. The stern of the boat opens to show a party and violent acrobatics during a storm at sea. Note the clown falling from the upper deck. (From *Trucs et Décor,* Paris, c. 1880.)

view.] Buildings and the boats at anchor vanish and little by little the horizon and the sea surround the vessel. The water ripples softly. Far away the sun is setting among flaming clouds when all of a sudden the stern of the packetboat opens up and one sees the passenger salon set up for dinner with everyone crowding around.

Soon the dining passengers stand up. Seats and tables disappear, carried out by servants. An entertainment is organized and couples dance to the strains of a waltz played by a pianist who spars with a piano placed at the back of the salon.

FIGURE 12. The storm-tossed vessel and the party were revisited in *Le Naufrage*, a three-act play at the Variétés. (From *Journal Quotidien*, Paris, September 10, 1885, in the Boston Public Library, Rare Books Department.)

The sun has set and the moon rises in the sky but the clouds begin to obscure it. Rumbling of thunder announces the approaching storm. The boat begins to roll with the mounting waves. The mast, funnel and bridge lean and right themselves.

The sea grows rougher and the waves get very high. Suddenly at a more violent blow, passengers turn head over heels on the floor and the pianist is pitched head first into the piano. A clowning passenger who has been perched on the gangway near the helmsman loses his balance and falls to the roof of the deckhouse which he breaks with a horrible crash and tumbles into a group of passengers.

FIGURE 13. The violence of the storm pitches the pianist head-long into the piano. (From *Trucs et Décor*, Paris, c. 1880.)

The lightning grows brighter, the thunder crashes more loudly and the wind blows in rage. The vessel is sinking! One sees the sailors lower the lifeboats after which the vessel appears to sink beneath the waves. The curtain falls on that effect.

The complex machinery necessary to stage this scene is described in detail by George Moynet. It was apparently the work of William Hanlon, who had patented a somewhat simpler version of the boat apparatus in the United States in 1882. (See Appendix B.)

In the fall of 1885, some Hanlons appeared in a three-act play entitled "Le Naufrage (Shipwreck) de M. Godet" at the Variétés.[8] This could only have been Edward and Frederick, who were Europe at the time. George and William were busy with *Fantasma* in New York.

Perhaps the most memorable Hanlon sketch was a showstopper in high-speed English pantomime cum acrobatics. It was a drunk scene which made the maximum use of *la trappe anglaise*, described later.

For this scene, a special box set, replete with 13 traps of every description and special equipment, was used. In one form or another it served the Hanlons in show after show for the rest of their career. It became a feature in the later Hanlon spectacular, *Fantasma*. A version without the drunk but using a similar box set was resurrected by George's son, George Jr., for the Broadway show *Hooray for What*, starring Ed Wynn in 1937.

Georges Moynet described the dazzling action in the original presentation:

The scene is a hotel room. A large man with white whiskers and a bald head is shown in by a domestic who turns down the bed and arranges the traveler's baggage. That person appears tipsy. To his questions, the housekeeper assures him the hotel is quiet and any disturbers will be immediately ejected.

The traveler pours a drink but awkwardly spills the water and as a result tosses off a full glass of whiskey under the envious look of the housekeeper. The drink is the finishing touch to the man's intoxication and he staggers about. He pushes out the housekeeper with the intention of putting himself to bed.

Our man takes off his overcoat and sits on the bed. There he takes off his boots with difficulty. The boots, once removed, walk across the floor as though they were on invisible legs. The drunk is amazed and throws himself on the fugitives but they escape. With a gesture he indicates to the audience that the wall of the room will stop them.

But no! The shoes climb the wall gracefully, each boot moving in turn and the unhappy owner, his eyes wide, watches them disappear into the ceiling.

He is puzzled. Mechanically he takes out a cigar and tries to light it with the candle on the nightstand. The candle is bewitched and avoids the cigar, flying away. The candle rises up to the picture of a woman hanging on the wall. The head of the woman turns into a devil's head and blows out the candle. The man throws away the cigar and decides to sleep in his clothes but the moment he lies on the mattress, he recoils in horror. The devil's head is lying on the pillow and yawning with an enormous mouth. The man grabs an umbrella and strikes at the form of the body.

The devil's form on the mattress disappears instantly but the head appears beneath the bed and two long arms grab the legs of the man just as he is congratulating himself on his apparent victory.

The man falls and the devil leaps out and bounds downstage. The audience sees his costume with black collar and silver ornaments. He goes over and sits on an armchair against the scenery at stage right. The drunk gets up with the umbrella and throws himself on the apparition only to hit the wall violently. The chair and the devil have disappeared. At the same instant at the opposite side of the stage the devil shoots up about 9 feet through a trap in the stage floor and lands on his hands. He sits down on a chair on the opposite side of the stage from the first chair.

The poor, persecuted drunk advances on his tormentor and the same action takes place. Chair and devil disappear and at the same instant, behind the drunk, the relentless devil shoots up through the stage floor and does a high bound.

The unhappy man chasing the black devil sees him near the back wall disappear and change into another devil in a white suit. The drunk now has a problem with two devils who pass and repass in a flash through all the openings in the scenery. At one point the black devil flies to the back scenery, and turns his back on the audience as he climbs the wall. At about 10 feet off the floor he moves like a giant spider, arms and legs extended and executes two or three revolutions as though he were looking for a route. He then resumes his climb and disappears into the ceiling.

As the chase continues the white devil enters a wardrobe and changes into a red devil. The housekeeper gets involved and the neighbors who have been awakened by the racket break into the room. The devils escape completely but the chase is replaced by an attempt to explain the problem which turns stormy and becomes a battle. Neighbors, housekeeper, hotel guests and the police kick, shove and beat each other. At one point an old woman is thrown out the window and the curtain falls on a general melee.[9]

The basic idea of this scenario was modified for the final act of *Le Voyage en Suisse*, to be described in the next chapter. There it was transformed into a grand chase between two servants and a gendarme.

As might be expected, "drunk scenes" or "The Haunted Hotel" were copied over and over by other artists. In 1903, Georges Méliès produced *The Inn Where No Man Rests,* a short film complete with a moving candle, boots that walk by themselves, and dancing bed, etc.

One of the time-honored stunts of English pantomimists was made possible by the invention of *la trappe anglaise,* as the French called it. A number of different mechanical arrangements came under this term, but all were trap doors which opened easily and shut instantly. A common form was two swinging doors on strong spring hinges. Another consisted of a number of rigid elastic belts, like two combs with their teeth meshed. These were usually mounted in the scenery and painted to match the wall. A star trap in the stage floor allowed a devil to fly into the air through apparently solid flooring.

These camouflaged openings made it possible for performers to vanish or appear through solid walls miraculously, providing the performer had the nerve for it. To exit, for example, required the clown or Harlequin to run headlong, leap and fly flat out through the hidden opening. Perfectly done, the performer vanished in a flash and scenery was undisturbed. It took abundant courage, split-second timing and great control. Among other things, the performer had to overcome the instinct to bend the knees lest he bash them as he went through. He also had to trust that a couple of stagehands were stationed behind the trap to catch him in a carpet. It was a job for acrobats, and no one was better prepared than the Hanlon Brothers.

The *trappe anglaise* and such daredevil gymnastics on the stage have not been seen for many years, but a hint can be seen in a stunt executed by Buster Keaton in his silent movie *Sherlock Jr.* In this scene an old lady peddler is standing against a brick wall, holding a tie tray. Keaton is being chased. On the dead run, he leaps headlong into the tray to hide and disappears utterly. The old lady walks away from the wall carrying her tie tray. There's no trace of where Keaton went. It was not movie magic, but took a highly skilled acrobat, a *trappe anglaise,* a limber old lady and a team behind the wall. Keaton's parents had no doubt seen the feat on the vaudeville stage.

The Hanlons' inventiveness during the Paris years pioneered a number of stage tricks that lived on. Half a century later, show business and magicians were consumed with legal battles over the "invention" and ownership of "Sawing a Woman in Half." One magician, Silent Mora, received many wires from Horace Goldin's lawyers demanding that he stop presenting the "Sawing."

Mora consulted a lawyer, General Harbord, a member of the president's cabinet. "[Harbord] listened to me describe the trick and then said, 'Mora, I saw that same illusion at the Folies Bergère years ago in Paris when I was taking a course at the University. It was shown by two clowns, named the Hanlon Brothers. Don't worry anymore!'"[10]

As a matter of record, a trick by a clown and harlequin separating a body into two pieces is described in Hopkins' *Magic*.[11]

~

CHAPTER FIVE

1879: Le Voyage en Suisse

By 1878, the Hanlon-Lees pantomimes were the top attraction at the Folies Bergère. After performances they would go to the Café du Gaulois, Montmartre, where they would meet newspaper writers, painters and musicians. A magazine of the times reported: "Here George Hanlon brews his singular night-cap. He takes a bowl of milk, beats up some yolks of eggs in it and pours in a half bottle of Medoc."

Among the Hanlons' fans they could count Émile Zola, Jules Verne, Jacques Offenbach, Henri Villemossant, editor of *Figaro,* and many more luminaries of Paris. Such was the popularity of the brothers that two clever writers, M. Blum and M. Toche, assigned to write a revue for the final year of the Variety Theatre, produced a caricature of the Hanlons with English actors mimicking their actions, their charm and some of their agility.

The English actors were very effective, and M. Bertrand, manager of the Variety, seeing the success of the copy, had the brilliant idea of replacing them with the originals. Accompanied by Offenbach, Bertrand approached the Hanlons with a proposal for an engagement at the Variety. A deal was struck.

The theatre commissioned Blum and Toche to write a full-length play specifically for the Hanlons. The Hanlons, of course, supplied acrobatics and mechanical inventions around which the plot and dialogue were woven. Much of the dialogue was in puns and rhyming couplets, all in French. Offenbach, who had suggested a comic opera, offered to compose the music but later confessed he was not able to keep pace with such nimble acrobats.

Thus was born *Le Voyage en Suisse* (The Trip to Switzerland), which premiered August 30, 1879, at the Théâtre des Variétés in Paris. It turned out to be the second great triumph of the Hanlons' career and played six months.

Le Voyage en Suisse was "perhaps one of the most significant productions in the history of popular entertainment, for in it a wide range of circus techniques, stage

FIGURE 14. The Hanlon-Lees Brothers: George and Frederick (*top*), William (*center*) and Edward and Alfred (*bottom*). Upon arrival in New York from Paris and London with *Le Voyage en Suisse*. (From *The New York Clipper*, November 5, 1881.)

music and dazzling trickwork was incorporated into a dramatic context and performed by a group of the world's most talented acrobats, jugglers and clowns."[1]

In France, Hanlon-Lees fans were enthralled, and intellectuals of the Naturalist movement hailed the clowns' pantomime as a perfect rendition of both reality and dream. Theodore de Banville was especially struck by the contrast between the grace and sweet innocence of their faces and their gymnastic ferocity.[2] Émile Zola was ecstatic. He praised the "cruel observations and cold-blooded analyses of these grinning clowns who laid bare, with a gesture or a wink, the entire human beast."[3]

In London, this "Parisian absurdity" was translated and adapted for the British audience by a Mr. Reece, who toned down the racier Parisian version so as not to offend British sensibilities. *Le Voyage en Suisse* was a farce in three acts and five tableaux, written purely to show off the unique talents of the Hanlon-Lees.

The play opens in a small village on the Devonshire coast, with a chorus of townspeople celebrating the coming wedding of the beautiful Julia to Finsbury Parker.

Into this happy occasion steps the elderly villain, Matthew Popperton, who arrives with a letter from Julia's guardian, Herr Schwindelwitz, who forbids the marriage and orders her back to his hotel in Switzerland, further commanding that if Popperton should propose to Julia she must accept. Schwindelwitz schemes to share Julia's fortune with Popperton.

Alone on the stage, the distraught Parker is heartened by the appearance of his uncle, Sir George Golightly, who promises to help Parker rescue Julia with the aid of Golightly's two nephews, Ned and Harry (Edward and George Hanlon). The two nephews, due to arrive from school at Bonn, are accompanied by their French tutor, M. La Chose (Agoust). The story is how Popperton is thwarted on the trip back to Switzerland.

The Hanlons' entrance is explosive. A huge carriage arrives, loaded with Sir George's two nephews, their tutor and a mountain of baggage. The coach, drawn by a live horse, is led by Popperton's two white-faced servants (Frederick and William Hanlon). Halfway across the stage the carriage overturns in a violent smash-up. Carriage, gentlemen, English trunks—everything is demolished into a hundred pieces. But to relieve the audience's horror, the Hanlon-Lees come sliding down the wreckage, landing in a perfect row at the footlights, calmly smoking cigars, with one brother sitting on another's shoulders.

In the next scene, the group repairs to a tavern, where a bravura juggling exhibition takes place. The two servants (William and Frederick) steal a bottle of brandy from a customer who ordered it. While the thirsty customer watches with suspicion, the servants, assisted by Agoust, pass the bottle from one to the other with such speed and precision that it is impossible to follow their moves. When the bottle is finally delivered, the brandy is gone. In another trick, a waiter is carrying a basket of champagne bottles across the room when one of the comics, who is handling a gun, lets it go off. Instantly the precious juice is spraying from the basket onto the floor. In reviews, this display of sleight of hand was singled out as one of the most excellent scenes of the show and praised for "absolute precision of execution" and "marvels of polished nicety and finish."

One report gives us some insight into the Hanlons' pantomimic technique. Speaking of the footmen (William and Frederick), "ideas dawn slowly on their

FIGURE 15. A horse-drawn carriage falls apart and scatters the occupants in an opening scene from *Le Voyage*. (From a color promotional booklet in the Boston Public Library, Rare Books Department.)

faces, both vacant as slates; by degrees they assume form and consistency and every feature is lighted up; the frame of each man is permeated by one idea. You can read it in every delicate modulation of gesture. It seems to absorb the entire being, to throb in every nerve, to quiver in every muscle. . . ."[4]

Act I ends with Julia, Popperton and his two servants leaving for Switzerland with Parker, M. La Chose, Golightly and his two nephews in pursuit to harass Popperton and prevent his proposal to Julia. Popperton's two servants, Bob and John (Frederick and William), are also enlisted in the effort.

Act II takes place in a stage version of a railroad sleeping car. Four compart-

FIGURE 16. With wheels spinning, the sleeping car speeds along toward Switzerland while the clowns use every trick to prevent a marriage proposal. (From a promotional booklet for *Le Voyage* in the Boston Public Library, Rare Books Department.)

ments are open to the audience, while underneath the wheels are spinning, giving the illusion of a train traveling at high speed. Popperton and Julia are in one compartment and the rest of the cast keep up a barrage of fast and furious intrusions to thwart Popperton's advances. The action takes place in each of the compartments and then all in one. Characters appear and disappear like magic through solid walls or the ceiling. One of the servants falls onto the tracks and slides along under the wheels only to reappear on the roof. They disguise themselves as conductors and customs inspectors to interrupt the couple. They bang on Popperton's door and call for quiet when the room is totally silent. Sir George plays a raucous solo on a trumpet. Not a minute goes by without some ploy to frustrate the evil suitor.

When the rescue team finally runs out of tricks, Golightly bribes a railroad guard to derail the train and blow it up. In the ensuing explosion the railroad car splits in two on the stage, blowing the terrified passengers safely into nearby trees.

In Act III the whole group arrives at Rigi Kulm Hotel with Popperton still seeking to propose to Julia. At a dinner there, Popperton's two servants set about serving and succeed in wrecking the hotel. They drop stacks of plates, spill a tureen of hot soup on a guest and upset a coffeepot on a waistcoat. A French general (Agoust) juggles oranges, loaves of bread, silverware and plates.[5]

To cap it off, one of the servants goes upstairs with a light to a room where dynamite is hidden. The explosion blows the servant through a hole in the ceiling and he falls on his back in the middle of the dining table, through which he passes.[6]

To open the final scene, the servants grow progressively more intoxicated, and in trying to light a candle, one thrusts the lit candle down the other's throat instead of the bottle. This episode captured the imagination of both French and English reviewers, who lavished high praise on it.

> But their highest achievement is a drunken scene. . . . In its way nothing could be better than this. It is so dreadfully true to nature and withal so genuinely diverting that one gazes on it with an enthralled interest which would be more fittingly applied to some burst of passion at the Lyceum.[7]

Zola had already pronounced that "nothing is more accurate nor complete than the fumbling of these two drunks dulled by wine who, wishing to have a light, lose successively the matches, the candle, the chandelier without ever once finding one of the objects. That is the total psychology of the drunk."[8]

A gendarme (Agoust), who suspects the servants of being responsible for the wreck of the train, enters and begins a mad chase to apprehend them. This last scene, one of the most applauded sketches in the drama, was an adaptation of the "Haunted Hotel" scene described in the last chapter. Like the devils, the servants elude the policeman by popping into and out of trunks, clocks, fireplace and staircase. Double doors on a wardrobe baffle their pursuer. When the gendarme crawls into a trunk, one of the servants stands on the lid, apparently slicing off his head. "Though the two are always hovering round their would-be captor," said a reviewer, "he could not once have detected their presence. He opens the door of a

FIGURE 17. Three servants (Hanlons) lead a gendarme (Agoust) on a wild chase filled with baffling pantomimic tricks. (From a color promotional booklet for *Le Voyage* in the Boston Public Library, Rare Books Department.)

cupboard, to which he has tracked one of the men who is there indeed, but who slips quietly through the legs of his adversary. . . . Some of the leaps and tricks tax the courage as well as the agility of these excellent mimes, but the absence of perceptible effort is always a source of pleasure to the spectator."[9]

The famous English impresario John Hollingshead saw *Le Voyage* at the Théâtre des Variétés and engaged the troupe for his Gaiety Theatre in London, where it opened March 27, 1880. As the Hanlons told it, one of the first to see the piece in Paris was the future King Edward, then the Prince of Wales. The Prince was fascinated by the mechanical effects and was invited by M. Bertrand to view the play on the stage behind the scenes. The Prince was quoted as having told George, "You must take this piece to London. I will arrange with Hollingshead." So, according to William, London first saw the play under the personal patronage of the Prince of Wales.[10]

London was high success all over again, and reviewers were enthralled by the Hanlons' skills at pantomime. "No description could help the reader enjoy their perfection of pantomimic devilment," was a typical report.[11]

The program says that music was composed and selected by Herr Carl Meyder. Music must have added a great deal to the flavor of Hanlon pantomimes, but we can find few clues to the actual music used in this or most other Hanlon productions.

The London engagement was marred by the abrupt departure of Agoust. Agoust later gave his story to the French press: The brothers had become envious of Agoust's salary and the fact that London and Paris reviewers frequently singled him out for special praise. They resolved to put him down in a scene. While he was playing the role of the gendarme, Agoust and others were attacked by the Hanlon clowns with heavy blows to the head with a giant barometer. When he realized that the blows were more violent than called for, Agoust drew his saber and shouted to the wings, "The first one who wounds me I will kill!" The audience didn't think it was any more than a joke, but the next day Agoust quit the troupe and became director of the Nouveau Cirque, Paris.[12]

There are plausible reasons for a growing strain between Agoust and the Hanlons. In their *Mémoires*, published the previous year, the Hanlons gave Agoust short shrift. His many contributions to their career were ignored, and mention was confined to a demeaning anecdote about a cruel trick they had played upon him.

Agoust was bitter, and the feeling festered for many years. About 1888 he complained to the Paris press that the *Mémoires* were not the true history of the Hanlons and omitted the important part that he had played ever since Thomas' death. He further claimed that George had been physically abusive to Thomas after his fall at Cincinnati. This story was picked up by *The New York Mirror* and a duel of heated letters between Agoust and the Hanlons ensued. (See Appendix A.)

The Hanlons denied the charge and defended themselves "against such outrageous falsities and by a man whom we were compelled to get rid of years ago." It was a sad postscript to what had been a highly productive relationship. Agoust ultimately left the Nouveau Cirque and toured with his family in a vaudeville sketch, "Un Restaurant Parisien," very much like the chaotic dinner scene in *Le Voyage.*

Even before the opening at the London Gaiety, the Hanlons' old manager, Morris Simmonds, sailed for Europe and signed up *Le Voyage en Suisse* for an American tour to begin the next season.[13]

Le Voyage opened at the Park Theatre in New York on September 12, 1881. Simmonds joined forces with Col. T. Allston Brown to manage the show, and again the script of the play was reworked, this time by Henry Pettitt.

After a few months in New York theatres, the show toured the entire country for an additional 82 weeks, never closing except for one day, after President Garfield was assassinated.

No one could match the vitality of the original *Le Voyage* when the Hanlons were in the cast, but it is interesting to note that Toche and Blum's script played on in Paris right through the turn of the century.

Once embarked on developing their next show, *Fantasma,* the Hanlons' interest in *Le Voyage* began to fade. In a letter to Colonel Brown, George said, "We are willing to sell 'Voyage' if you can find a cash purchaser." Years later, rights were sold to the Byrnes Brothers, a competitive troupe of acrobatic comics who used pieces of the show, but the Hanlons retained the right to stage the full play when they pleased.

Edward saw no place for himself in the new show and left for Spain, where he produced *Le Voyage* with Spanish talent. After playing Barcelona and Madrid, his show toured Europe, visiting Vienna, Hamburg, and other cities for about three years. Frederick joined Edward for a short time, but his poor health became serious and he died of consumption at Nice on April 6, 1886. Frederick was not really a Hanlon but was of Irish descent. Born at Leverton, Liverpool, he was apprenticed at an early age to Tom Hanlon, Senior, who adopted him. Beyond being a consummate acrobat and pantomimist, Frederick was an expert cyclist who had won many awards. He was also noted for his great linguistic abilities.

Earlier, Alfred had fallen ill shortly after *Le Voyage* opened in New York and was sent west by his brothers to recuperate. He did not recover and died on January 24, 1886, aged 44, in Pasadena, California. It was the end for the youngest of the trio which had debuted as "Entortilationists" and toured the world as children. Alfred, a musician, had composed many pieces and had managed the musical background for a number of the early pantomimes.

These premature deaths left just three of the original brothers, George, William and Edward, to carry on the Hanlon tradition for another three decades.

CHAPTER SIX

1884: Fantasma

As the three-year American tour of *The Trip to Switzerland* wound down, the Hanlons began preparing a new show. Their summers were spent on the seacoast at Cohasset, Massachusetts, which had become a popular resort for actors and show people. At first they had no suitable quarters, so the Hanlons rehearsed in a peach orchard what was promised to be "The Most Popular and Pleasing of all Spectacular Pantomimes."

There had been a lull in pantomimes on the American stage. The Ravel family had been popular favorites in the early years of the century. The superb comic George Fox had followed with an American-style *Humpty-Dumpty*, but he was gone. Some huge spectaculars such as *Aladdin* and *Cinderella* were produced with elaborate stage magic both in England and the United States.[1] *The Trip to Switzerland* had been written to show off the Hanlons' unmatched acrobatics and superb pantomimic skills. It was tremendously successful, but by 1884 George was nearly 50 years of age and William 45. The idea of managing a show, hiring new acts and taking less strenuous parts themselves was very attractive. The fairy spectacular was a format that could be revised every season and readily toured.

Fantasma was a potpourri of fairy tale, a struggle between good and evil, many pieces of stage magic, effects borrowed from past panto successes, specialty acts, much clowning and comedy, and—of course—transformations. The play concluded with a harlequinade.

The show was not exclusively pantomime. Fantasma, the Fairy Queen, disguised as a witch, and Zamaliel, king of Hades, an evil one, both actually spoke lines. Zamaliel's imp attendants were named Bathos, Hazzard, Ichtyo and Zarzar. Pico, a Clown, was obviously derived from the bumbling Pierrot. Farmer Close was the Old Man, or Pantaloon, father of Lena, or Columbine. Arthur, in love with Lena, was the show's Harlequin. Most of the story was told in dumb show but one purist reviewer questioned the use of a chorus of mixed voices as being inappropriate for pantomime.

Into this show the Hanlons crowded "tableaux of American pictures, the rough and tumble of English harlequinade, the French humor of a garden which grows human heads instead of cabbages, the Italian grotesqueries of a clown who plays the fiddle in impossible positions and a Harlequin who fights a broadsword combat with five ruffians."[2] All this was packed into two hours and 30 minutes. The show was put together with all the skill the Hanlons had learned during their many Paris successes.

When *Fantasma* premiered at the Fifth Avenue Theatre in New York on November 11, 1884, the full billing was:

THE HANLONS'
New Spectacular
FANTASMA!
Or, Funny Frolics in Fairyland
Presented by their Great Italian Pantomime Company

"Those who are familiar with the Continental methods of doing pantomimes will hear with pleasure that nothing yet seen in this country has so closely approached foreign methods . . . the cast of pantomimists proper are entirely new to America."[3] Indeed, the cast listed in the programs included 13 signoras, monsignoras and a signorina, presumably imported, but the *New York Clipper* noted that two Hanlons were present on the stage "in costume and under new stage names."[4]

Curiously, G. D. C. Odell reports a quite different cast for the Fifth Avenue Theatre premiere.[5] According to him, George appeared as Arthur and William as Father Close. Little Alice Hanlon, Little Frances Hanlon and four Zanfrettas were also in the cast. Alex Zanfretta played Pico. In fact, this was part of the cast for the next season, 1885–86. All mention of a "Great Italian Pantomime Company" had vanished. And lest there be any doubt, the program included the line "Invented, Arranged & Produced under the personal supervision and positive [personal] appearance of the Hanlon Brothers."

A reviewer of the premiere listed the novel effects he could remember: ". . . a demon dropping out of the clouds to make havoc in a rustic village, a witches' chariot, a new kind of magic bell, a lifelike bull with a penchant for breaking and entering, a bridge with a convenient trap for drowning the clown, a real stage cyclone, a devil's garden wherein cabbages change to human heads, a mysterious couch which manufactures occupants to order, a transportable grate-fire with the happy faculty of placing itself under the drowsy clown's nether parts. . . ."[6]

The sure-fire drunk scene with vanishing chairs, wandering shoes and candle, and a devil ascending the wall was reworked to take place in the Devil's Dormitory.

After a demon sleigh ride, the first act finale was a series of tableaux representing the progress of all nations in North Pole explorations, America's being the most distinguished.

Arthur's "sword combat with four antagonists—all attacking him at once—caused a perfect furor among the male portion of the audience."[7] This was a specialty originated by the actor Louis Pizzarello at the Paris Hippodrome and was to be included in *Fantasma* for several years.

The realistic cyclone of Act I, which tore up houses and left the stage a shambles, was used for one of the *Fantasma* posters. (See Plate 5.) Four years later, that scene was replaced by a deluge with rushing waters and the destruction of a village. The stage had the appearance of being entirely flooded with water.

At the end of Act II, Zamaliel is vanquished and Fantasma triumphs, leading to the transformation of characters into a Grand Harlequinade for Act III. The show concluded with the "Magnificent Transformation to Fantasma's Realm," a fairyland, of course.

As the show returned year after year, it was rewritten to introduce new tricks, spectacles and cast members. It was usually billed as "The New *Fantasma*," but many scenes remained.

Beginning with the 1887 *Fantasma*, "Bottom of the Sea" became one of the perennial features of the show. Behind a drop of green scrim was a setting of underwater grottos and giant rocks covered with shells. Calcium lights from the wings turned the scene into the depths of the sea. On the bottom, the fair Lena (actually a dummy "cleverly counterfeiting her appearance") was in the grasp of Zamaliel. From above, brave Arthur swam down in the murky depths to search for Lena. The illusion of swimming was accomplished by having Arthur ascend to the flies and put on a saddle-like leather belt attached to a wire. Stage hands lowered the swimming figure. When Arthur reached the ocean floor, imps emerged from submarine caves to aid Zamaliel in a violent duel with the earthling.[8]

Over the years this popular interlude was elaborated. Mermaids swam among the grottos. Huge sharks and other menacing sea creatures were introduced. The underwater scene reached a peak when a giant octopus appeared and filled the entire proscenium of the theatre. The octopus with its waving tentacles grasped Zamaliel and his imps and stuffed them in its mouth to the great delight of young audiences.

The Hanlons' love of violent clowning was not missing. An 1888 review describes some of the action:

There had been a stone wall in view. Zip! Whiz! Splash! and poor Pico, the white-faced, Pico the simple, Pico the much abused, sprawls upon the stage coming with as much ease and with a great deal more gusto than one ordinarily enters double doors or a big porte-cochere. Pico recovers from the momentary shock, then pulls himself together and looks about to discover who it was that fired him through the wall. No one about but a poor old man hobbling along as best his rheumaticky legs would carry him. Without more ado, Pico seizes the

FIGURE 18. To free Lena, Arthur swims down to duel with Zamaliel and his imps. (From a promotional booklet for *Fantasma* in the Harvard Theatre Collection, Houghton Library.)

poor old man and throws him out of the window. A crash of glass! Bump, bump, bumpety bump! And we can see in our mind's eye the poor inoffensive cripple falling many stories, from one roof to another upon the pavement below. Pico's white face and staring black eyes wrinkle up in silent laughter and he slaps his knee with a resounding smack, convulsed with the ludicrousness of the thing until he happens to bump into Zamaliel, the terrible king of the Realm of Heads.

Zamaliel frowns an awful frown and poor Pico shrivels up into a quaking penitent. So the play goes. Pico tries to follow his master Arthur through the most terrible regions of the beings with the heads, claws, tails and wings of animals always in pursuit of the beautiful daughter of Farmer Close, Lena, the fair.

FIGURE 19. The giant octopus grows to fill the proscenium and swallow the villains. (From a promotional booklet for *Fantasma* in the Harvard Theatre Collection, Houghton Library.)

She is seized by the devil, or rather Zamaliel, and the pursuers are aided by sweet Fantasma, the fairy. But aided by the good genius or thwarted by the evil one, poor, stupid Pico is bound to get into all the trouble there is.[9]

In this edition of *Fantasma,* Pico was played by François X. Zeltner, a French Swiss who was a clown on the continent before coming to this country and was with the original *Humpty-Dumpty* company which George Fox formed.

Another reviewer describes another scene in this same show:

The Skeleton Pass, another clever piece of mechanism, reveals a number of skeletons into whose midst poor Pico has accidentally fallen and who make the most of his presence [with] all sorts of pranks, winding up with a prize fight . . . capitally done, the positions, and movements of the arms . . . arranged by some-one well up on the manly art.[10]

The skeleton pugilists were life-size marionettes, manipulated on a stage draped entirely in black.

Following the skeleton scene, a dozen or so bears chase Pico into a log hut which they demolish, leaving only the chimney standing with Pico perched on top. When Pico sets off on a rabbit hunt, the elusive rabbit scuttles off with the sportsman's gun.

Along the way, Father Close gets a shower bath and Pico invents a novel way to pump him out. Unseen by the audience, a man behind a painted wall pumps water through a rubber tube which the farmer holds near his mouth.

The reviewer continues:

Probably the most striking and original scene in "Fantasma" is the "Grotto of the Magic Fountain," a combination of beautiful colors and handsome faces. A novel feature in this scene, invented by the Hanlons, is the revolving tableau. At a given signal about thirty ladies on pedestals including a fountain of statuesque figures, are seen to revolve noiselessly. The effect is extremely beautiful.[11]

From its premiere in 1884, *Fantasma* played steadily each season until 1890, when *Superba,* the new Hanlon show, was unveiled. During this period, William, being fully occupied with producing and managing, gave up performing. There-after *Fantasma* was seen only occasionally until about 1912. Even so, the Hanlons continued to add new tricks and bits of business to keep *Fantasma* fresh and up to date.

In 1895 William introduced a decapitation act in the show. (See Appendix B.) Pico, condemned to die, places his neck on a black block. The headsman swings a broad axe and it hits the block with a resounding thunk! Pico's head falls to the ground and "brings shrieks of horror from the feminine portion of the audience."[12]

To keep up with the times, in a 1905 edition of *Fantasma,* an enormous trunk was carried in on the shoulders of a little bit of a woman. At mid-stage, the sides of the trunk dropped over her and become an automobile with a real man in it. It was an echo of the mechanical transformations introduced into English pantomimes about the time William Hanlon was born.

Shortly after it was clear that *Fantasma* was a success, George, William and Edward made Cohasset their permanent summer headquarters and theatrical workshop. William bought a modest one-and-a-half story Cape Cod home on Jerusalem Road and promptly raised it in the air on blocks so that a substantial first floor could be built beneath it.

The next project was to create "The Hanlon's Scenic Studio." The first building was two stories in one section and three stories in the other, 65 feet high. It covered an area 80 by 100 feet. To townspeople it looked like a grain elevator, but it housed a complete stage, the largest paint frame in the country, dressing rooms, wardrobe rooms, wings, flies, etc. Later, two more buildings would be added for manufacture and storage of scenes, props and costumes. The facilities were complete with a railroad siding because the show could fill several baggage cars when it moved out in the fall.

Here in Cohasset, a cast and crew of up to 200 would spend the period from June to September hard at work preparing for the new season. William wisely made sure his staff enjoyed their work and saw to it that when they were not rehearsing, they had time for recreation. He encouraged swimming and fishing in the Atlantic Ocean.

William was acknowledged to be the inventive genius behind the productions and believed in hiring the best talent available. Top scene designers and performers came to Cohasset at his request. He even imported the Bruton family of papier-mâché specialists from England to make the grotesque properties. Robert Bruton, who had been at the London Drury Lane, his wife and two sons stayed with the Hanlon shows for many years, sometimes as performers, sometimes as property managers.

It was from this idyllic studio/plant that the second great "pantomimic spectacular," *Superba,* emerged.

CHAPTER SEVEN

1890: Superba

In its first year, *Superba* met with mixed reviews. When the play reached the Brooklyn Academy of Music in November 1890, *The New York Times* rendered a sour judgment on the story but a grudging appreciation of some of the scenery and trickwork. Fortunately, the review left us with a neat synopsis of the plot.

> The story of "Superba" is the old one of the incomprehensible and at times unintelligible admixture of fairies and mortals. Leander and Sylvia are mortals and they love. Wallawalla is a bad fairy who loves Leander, and for that reason seeks to separate him from Sylvia. But Leander is a true lover and withstands right nobly all her blandishments. Then Wallawalla resorts to magic, and with the aid of sprites, elves and hobgoblins, and other terrible creatures is about to carry her point when Superba with a great force of good magical people comes to the rescue of the lovers. A series of events follows, in which the good fairy and the bad fairy alternate in victory until at last Superba triumphs and Leander and Sylvia are united in love and happiness for all time.[1]

It is probable that some audiences, like the reviewer, had little patience with the fairy story and endured it only to see the tricks.

> The thread of this story wends a tortuous way through many strange lands, and is interwoven with many wonderful incidents, a vast majority of which have been made familiar to theatre-goers by their frequency on the stage in other productions of the Messrs. Hanlon. Of course, there are a white-faced clown, an idiotic bumpkin, and a short-skirted soubrette. The merriment of the entertainment depends upon these and is always extremely mild.
> The display of scenery, however, is good, with the exception of the transformation, and there are a floral ship effect and a balloon ascension that are unusually fine. Another scene wherein flowers unfolded and revealed the faces of the

fairies also found much favor with the spectators. But the costumes were ordinary and the supernumerary force of women was mediocre in appearance and ability to entertain.[2]

Be that as it may, *Superba* went on to become an annual event in leading theatres across the nation, enjoyed by old and young alike for over 20 years and occasionally breaking box office records. It is true that the Hanlons hung on to some panto tricks and sketches that had proved their worth over the years, but this was an era in which acts appearing before a few hundred people at a time could spend a lifetime with the same material. Only later would television grind up acts by appearing before many millions at a single showing. In *Superba*'s day, audiences could stand to see, over and over, sight comedy that had been honed to near-perfection in years of performance.

As a matter of fact, *Superba* could always justly proclaim "all new this season." The off-season in Cohasset was devoted to building new props, painting new scenery and, most importantly, devising new tricks, mostly the work of William, who knew what delighted audiences most.

Superba was produced to give the remaining brothers a rest from the rigors of performing in as many as ten shows a week. George was 55, William 51 and Edward 44. For the first ten years of *Superba*, no Hanlons appeared in the cast, but every season brought changes with new soubrettes, corps de ballet, Tiller girls and, especially, the best specialty acts William could hire. One can only imagine the standards the Hanlons would insist on for acrobats. The Filippi Family, The Four Schrode Brothers and Charles Guyer were variety headliners who were woven into *Superba*.

From newspaper accounts, albeit sketchy, and from patent papers it is possible to decipher some of the cryptic titles given the action in the playbills. The "floral ship effect" referred to by the *Times* reviewer was usually listed as "The Fairy Ship on a Sea of Roses." It was a grand transformation often used to end the show. Fred Hanlon, a son of George, described the effect many years later in an article of reminiscences.

> Twenty successive gauzes [scrim] were raised, each disclosing fresh beauty, like a great kaleidoscope, until with the raising of the last, a big ship whose hull was made of coloured glass of different colours, on which the lights flashed and made them into jewels, seemed to be sailing over real water towards the audience, its sail and rigging made of roses. Other rose craft came to meet it and escort it in. The audiences went wild.[3]

From one of their early Parisian pantomimes, a show-stopping trick was resurrected: "The Magic Mirror." The concept actually predated the Hanlons and was a staple effect in pantos of the 18th century. It served the Hanlons well over the years and was still a feature of the Hanlons' act when the sons of George were performing at the Folies Bergère, long after *Superba* was no more. The magician Silent Mora described "The Magic Mirror" as he had seen it performed when he was a child.

> I recalled that wonderful piece of teamwork portrayed by two clowns in "Superba" where after the mirror is "accidently" broken, one clown stands in front of the mirror while the other is directly in back of it. The movements of their hands and bodies work in perfect synchronism giving the impression of "mirror reflection" until the clown in front strikes a match and lights it while the clown in back has to strike twice to get a light. It had all been so perfectly done . . . when the illusion was spoiled . . . the element of surprise was so great the audience burst into laughter and applause.[4]

This pantomimic tour de force has been imitated over and over by succeeding clowns and comics, but—as Mora said—"never to such degree of perfection as was presented by the Hanlon Brothers."

As part of the story, Wallawalla orders the execution of Sylvia. The condemned girl is seated on the "Execution Chair," which is raised to the shoulders of four men. The men stand directly in the center of the stage near the footlights. At the back of the stage, a considerable distance away, lights are shining brightly. A hood is thrown over the girl while preparations are being made for her execution. Superba appears to rescue her. A moment later the hood is raised and the girl has vanished.[5] This illusion was patented by William (see Appendix B), as was the following:

Pierrot in the costume of a knight is seated in a high-backed chair. A vengeful character, uttering threats, approaches with a sword. Pierrot, flailing his legs, arms and head, tries to ward off the attack and demonstrates that he is a real person. Nevertheless, the attacker first severs the knight's legs with his sword and sets them aside. He then lops off the moving arms and drops them to the floor. Finally he cuts off the obviously living head and raises it off the neck. A curtain is drawn over the scene and the attacker moves down front to boast about his feat. As he does so the knight just seen dismembered crosses in front of his attacker and goes off stage. (See Appendix B.)

The Great Railroad Scene, an "intricate mechanical effect" filled the entire stage and included six locomotives huffing and puffing, with one monster engine

PLATE 1. The cover of a color promotional booklet for *The New Fantasma*, a "grand fairy spectacular." (From the Harvard Theatre Collection, Houghton Library.)

PLATE 2. The "Haunted Hotel," where nightmares plague the poor traveler, was a revised version of the Hanlons' famous "drunk scene" of an earlier pantomime. (From a color promotional booklet for *Fantasma* in the Harvard Theatre Collection, Houghton Library.)

PLATE 3. Poster for *Le Voyage en Suisse*. (From the New York Public Library for the Performing Arts.)

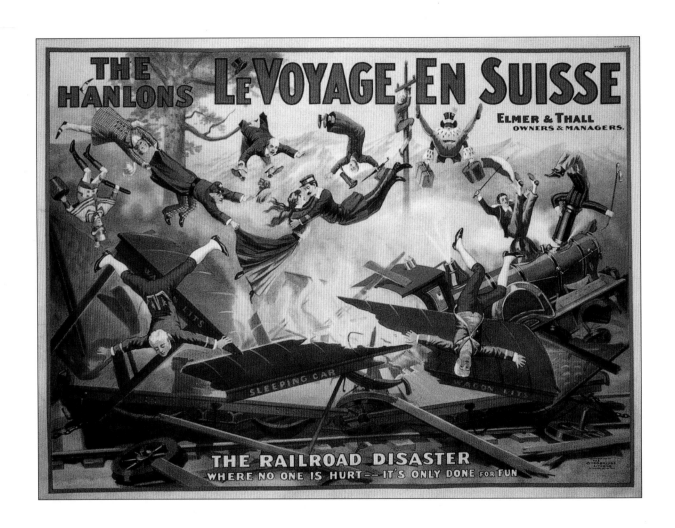

PLATE 4. Poster of the "Railroad Disaster" in *Le Voyage en Suisse*. (Through the courtesy of Ricky Jay.)

PLATE 5. Poster of the "Great Cyclone" in *Fantasma*. (From the New York Public Library for the Performing Arts.)

PLATE 6. The Hanlon-Lees in "Do Mi Sol Do" at Folies Bergère, with Agoust as maestro. (Through the courtesy of Ricky Jay.)

PLATE 7. Poster of the "Card Game in the Whale" in *Superba*. (Through the courtesy of Ricky Jay.)

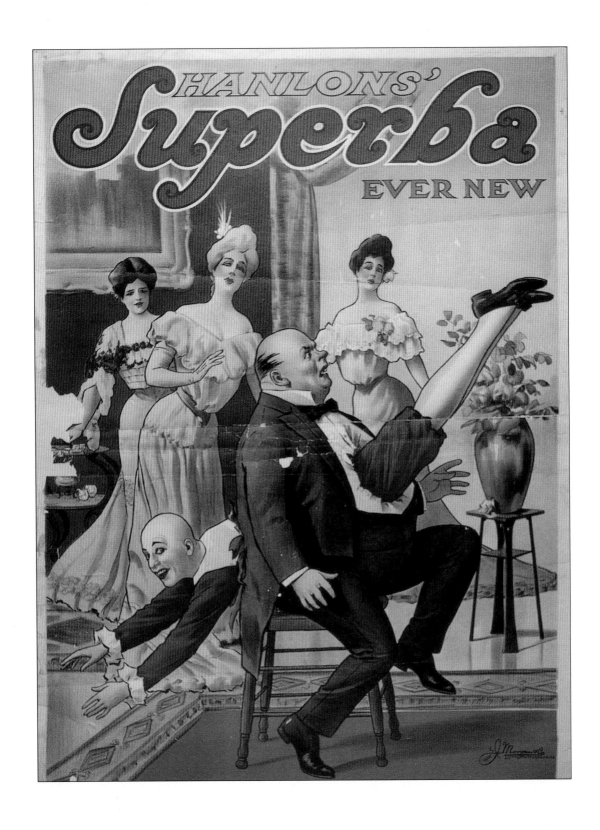

PLATE 8. Poster of "Pico Plunges through a Stuffed Shirt" in *Superba*. (From the New York Public Library for the Performing Arts.)

with a blazing headlight heading straight at the audience. As the gigantic engine came steaming over the footlights, and out over the heads of those in the front rows, children ran screaming up the aisle and it was some time before they could be induced to go back to their seats. The orchestra men heightened the illusion by all ducking for safety.[6]

Another of William's patents was the ludicrous "Educated Horse." A horse led on stage was seen to have a head on both ends and a rider who faced in both directions. Who knows what ribald pantomime ensued? (See Appendix B.)

In the "Useful Man" or "The Walking Hotel," Joe Filippi, who played the part of a valet, enters with his master, a tourist. The valet is dressed in ordinary clothes. The tourist is overcome by drowsiness and looks about for a place to sleep. The climax to the scene comes when a folded bed, heretofore unseen, drops from the valet's shoulders. The bed has legs strong enough to take the master's weight and he promptly lies down and goes to sleep.

"Bottom of the Sea," first featured in *Fantasma,* apparently took on a more benign air. A poster of the time depicts three sailors playing cards in the belly of a whale. The staple drunk scene lived on in the form of Pierrot's nightmare.

All these things were seen in the 1894–95 edition of *Superba.*

When *Superba* was in its second year, a major change took place in the relationship of the brothers. George suddenly and mysteriously renounced show business and joined the church. George was known to be deeply religious. One account asserts that he became a Presbyterian minister. Years later, one of his sons wrote that his father had bought an estate at Troy, N.Y., to bring up his children.

In the same year that George departed, the show sustained a major blow. As *Superba* was about to begin an engagement in Cleveland, the Euclid Avenue Opera House burned to the ground and all scenery and props, new for the season, were lost. It was October and the show had only been on the road for four weeks. The Hanlons were on their way to the insurance office when the fire broke out. There wasn't a cent of insurance. The cast suffered even worse, losing their costumes, which were their personal property, and their clothing, none of it insured. William and Edward assured the cast that they would be taken care of.[7]

At the time of the fire, the Hanlons claimed this year's show had cost $25,000 and couldn't be replaced on short notice for less than $60,000. It would be impossible to replace the show before April, they said. As a matter of fact, *Superba* was booked into the 14th Street Theatre in New York for Christmas.

Superba continued to make its annual tour, "all new this season." New scenes, new transformations, new rewrites of the book were offered to keep the theatres filled. A Chicago newspaper observed:

"Superba" was originally intended to be a pantomime in which the silent clown, with gestures and facial contortions, graphically describes his wants, and by dumb show performs many amusing feats but "Superba" is a pantomime no longer; each year so much has been added to it in a scenic way that it has eventuated into a spectacle. All the old scenery has been discarded and new and more elaborate has replaced it. Majestic baronial halls, mountainous passes, Oriental interiors that would grace a Sultan's harem, and glimpses into fairyland. It is uniquely interlarded with clever character songs, the newest ballads, dialectic imitations, graceful acrobatic feats and comic eccentricities of various sorts.[8]

Perhaps so, but William was still in charge, and one of the "comic eccentricities" in later shows was The Human Stove, first seen in *Fantasma*. A man ordinarily dressed comes out on stage. Beneath his waistcoat, handy for the woman who works the act with him, is a fire. Protecting it are two grate-bars. A pot is put on the fire to boil and eggs are cooked for the lady's supper. She wishes to do her ironing and puts an iron on to heat in the center of the man's tummy. The fire is real, yet the man suffers no discomfort.[9]

There continued to be startling and unexpected stunts for Pierrot, who was sometimes called Coco, sometimes Pico, but was always bumbling and in trouble. As a Hanlon clown did in a pantomime of 1875, Pierrot might, without warning, shoot skyward in a train of sparks like a meteor and disappear into the flies.

Shortly after the turn of the century, George Hanlon apparently had a change of heart and returned to show business. He had been gone for about ten years and now resided in Troy, N.Y., which would suggest that a serious rift had occurred with William and Edward, who remained at Cohasset. George's only comment was the cryptic statement, "I left on principle and I returned on principle." About 1901, the Hanlon name began appearing once again among *Superba*'s cast of characters. George's sons Fred and George W., Jr. were first. Then George, Sr., George, Jr., Fred, William II, Alfred Hanlon and John H. Haslam all appeared in a 1903 version of the show.

On January 2, 1906, scenery and props for *Superba* were again destroyed in the Globe Theatre fire at Boston. There was no insurance, but *Fantasma* was always available to cover the time until *Superba* could be rebuilt. George, Sr. and family continued in *Fantasma*.[10]

This revival introduced a new transformation, "The Lustrous Land Where the Bubbles Blow," as a finale. A reviewer describes the scene:

. . . curtain after curtain rise to reveal new beauties of coloring and design and the picture becomes more and more dazzling. Handsomely costumed women appear from hidden recesses and finally hundreds of bubbles float up against the background of flowers in the center of which is a large globe with a maiden enthroned upon it.[11]

This large bubble was the invention of George W., Jr. (see patent in Appendix B). It was later used in a vaudeville sketch together with the popular song "I'm Forever Blowing Bubbles," while the girl was seen floating inside the bubble.

The ancient act of shadow pictures was resurrected and used in both *Fantasma* and *Superba.* It had served the Hanlons well when they were fumbling for acts to replace acrobatics, and now, a generation later, it proved to be a hilarious novelty. On a full-stage white screen, silhouetted characters appeared running swiftly on the hunt for Pico.

> Pico comes running toward the audience, growing larger and larger with each step and to all appearances he just steps from the stage and disappears in the balcony. Presently the clown leaps down from some hidden place and runs away growing smaller and smaller. One by one the others follow growing smaller and smaller until they are mere pygmies. Around and around they go changing size, leaping into space and back again with wonderful swiftness. In this amusing pantomime they are appropriate and consequently make a hit.[12]

The return of George and his sons was obviously the "last hurrah" on the stage for George, who was now 71. It didn't last long, and thereafter he was listed as stage manager, if at all.

While William and Edward were always listed as proprietors and managers, the day-to-day management of *Superba* was in the hands of George's sons Fred and William II, who saw to it that the show continued to tour until 1911.

In the final months of *Superba,* a reviewer, sensing perhaps that the end was near, summed up the work of Pico:

> Almost the only thing we have left in the way of pantomime is Hanlon's "Superba," now making its appearance at the Bastable. It retains what it has had since the beginning of its long career, a front rank position among entertainments whose delight depends upon the eye . . .
>
> The show is pantomime and we hope it will continue to be so. Pico the clown comes down from the moon. Magic attends him. Great animals bounce out at him. Nothing that he tries to lay hold of is where he thinks it is. Fair maidens beckon him and when he would fain implant chaste salutes upon their ruby lips there is nothing but a rock or a wall; or worse still, the gaping mouth of some scaly monster or hellish demon. He will drink and the bottle is whisked out of his hands and goes flying toward the moon. He will go upstairs and when

he has done so, the stairs disappear and leave him on the lintel, pounding on a second story which gives him no reply.

He looks at his reflection in the mirror and goes through the antics of satisfaction as the rest of us sometimes do when we think we are alone; but when he tries to light his cigar the match goes out and he stands jabbering in fear watching his reflection which has his cigar cheerfully burning.

Pico is Fred Hanlon and William Hanlon II and their act, more particularly in the mirror scene, is of a high order of pantomime. Surrounded as they are with stage accessories and machinery which have been evolved from a generation of experience and supported not only by a company of capable pantomimists and acrobats on the stage but also by a big force of hardworking magicians in overalls behind the scenes, the entertainment they give deserves the steady support which audiences are always ready to supply.[13]

CHAPTER EIGHT

The Other Hanlons

ANYONE ATTEMPTING TO TRACE the careers of the Hanlon brothers is certain to run into a sea of confusion caused by billings and news items for acrobats under the name of Hanlon: Hanlon Brothers, Hanlon-Voltas, Hanlon-Volter-Martinetti.

Not generally explained is the fact that in the early years, the Hanlons took on a number of pupil apprentices, teaching them all they knew about acrobatics. It began in the 1860s when Thomas was impressed by the antics of three little Irish boys in a Westminster street. They were cousins named Carmody, O'Mara and Carey. Thomas saw to their training, and Carmody became "Little Bob" and one of the Hanlon Midgets.

In some cases the children were adopted by the family. As we have seen, these recruits appeared on stage with the Hanlons from time to time under a variety of names: the Hanlon Midgets, Master George, Master Bob, Little Bob, Julian, Victor and Robert. Little Bob continued to appear with the *Frères Hanlon-Lees* at the Folies Bergère as late as 1872.

In later years, some of the proteges struck out on their own but retained the Hanlon name. Eventually Carmody and O'Mara were associated with the Volta Brothers to become the Hanlon-Volta team, which was an attraction for many years at the London Crystal Palace under the management of Mr. Wieland. Their stupendous rigging extended across the entire roof of the transept, 100 feet from the ground and 80 feet from the net.

Little Bob in particular was a superb trapeze performer. Even as a child when he performed in the Hanlons' "Leap for Life" act, he would climb higher than William or George. He died in London on June 30, 1907.

However, it became annoying when the theatrical press frequently confused these younger "Hanlons" with the original group. When William (O'Mara), one of the Hanlon-Volter-Martinetti group, fell from a trapeze at the Academy of

Music in August 1890, the reports mistakenly identified him as one of the original Hanlons who performed "Zampillaerostation" at Niblo's Gardens.

A letter signed by George, William and Edward, complaining about the report, was promptly published in the *Dramatic Mirror* and explained that Robert and William of the Hanlon-Volter-Martinetti combination had started as apprentices to brother Thomas and were not the original Hanlons, "nor Hanlons at all." This last may have been a bit of overstatement by the three brothers, inasmuch as the boys had been adopted.

Actually it had been 20 years or more since any of the original brothers had performed on the trapeze, and at the time they were deeply involved in producing *Superba*. Nevertheless, when William (O'Mara) broke his neck the following year in another fall while performing with the Forepaugh Circus in Iowa, he was again misidentified as one of the brothers who had produced *Fantasma*. The newspaper notice concluded, "Two Hanlons still survive and will continue with the circus." The two "brothers" were Robert, who had been Little Bob, and a James "Hanlon" who had never had any association with the Hanlon family.

Since the name Hanlon had long had a powerful mystique in the world of acrobatics, there were other groups who simply appropriated the name. As late as 1911, Fred Hanlon, a son of George, complained to *Variety* that the La Dent Trio had become the "Three Hanlons."

CHAPTER NINE

~

The Later Years

THE HANLONS' *Superba* finally closed about 1912 after a run of 20 years. The story was beginning to wear thin, but the show remained popular right to the very end. In one of its last seasons, an Atlanta reviewer observed:

"Superba," as spectacular as ever, was presented to a top-heavy house at the Lyric Monday night . . . the whole house appreciated the spectacular part of the show. Rarely has there been a show to play at popular prices which carries the amount of scenery this show does and every bit of it worked just at the right moment. In fact the scenery should have been featured in the present production.[1]

Eventually, the rights to this and *Fantasma* reputedly were sold off to a theatrical family named Holly and changed hands more than once. None lasted long.

Sometime in the 1880s, the title to *Le Voyage en Suisse* had been sold to the Byrne Brothers, who had long imitated the Hanlons with shows such as *Eight Bells*. From that point, the Byrnes had the right to produce such scenes as the storm at sea with the sinking boat and the overturned carriage. They took out patents on their own versions.

Even before *Fantasma* and *Superba* were making their final appearances, William, Jr. and Fred, sons of George, were embarking on a vaudeville act of their own, *Just Phor Phun*. This was mostly pantomimic features drawn from the big Hanlon shows: the Mirror Magic, the Decapitation, the Haunted Hotel and the like were worked into sketches which Fred and Will performed around the world in vaudeville, night clubs and variety halls, just as their father and uncles had done many years before. In 1913 they were headlining in Paris at the Alhambra in *The Haunted Hotel*. Thirty years later they were still working as clowns and joined Ringling Brothers, Barnum and Bailey circus in 1945. As a lifelong performer, Fred has left some record of the almost lost art of pantomime.

73

There are few real pantomimists working now. Men will not give up the time necessary for perfection, without which the act is dead. As tiny kids, my brothers and I were kept at work. We loved it and long before we were allowed out on the stage, we used to attempt all sorts of tricks in private.

How is mere dumb show prepared? Many people might think that much of it is impromptu. Nothing could be wider of the mark. A script was prepared down to the dialogue—for the actor, though he does not speak, must seem to be articulating the words and it is only by knowing the actual speeches that the actor can get his real meaning across the footlights. Every single gesture must be studied and brought down to a second's delivery. Though emotion in pantomime is exaggerated, rehearsal is carried on by means of more natural expressions. Often my father would pull us up for grimacing in too exaggerated a form. It took strenuous rehearsal before he was satisfied. We spent hours in front of a mirror trying to master a new twist that would express an emotion.[2]

As we have seen, George W., Jr. had long been inventing spectacular stage effects such as his giant bubble. In 1914 he contracted with Flo Ziegfeld for the introduction of a motion picture illusion in the Follies.

In the same year he arranged for the Edison Motion Picture Company to produce a five-reel adaptation of *Fantasma,* which was released in time for the holidays.[3] George played Pico, the clown in the film. Sadly, only one reel survives in the archives of the Library of Congress, and unfortunately it is the first reel. As a prologue, it contains none of the stunts or scenes and mechanical illusions which made *Fantasma* so memorable.

However, a detailed script for the film version was preserved and leaves a scene-by-scene record. It is evident that George packed in every possible sketch from years of *Fantasma* productions with special emphasis on Pico's role. The script specifies every pantomimic move, but even a brief outline of the last two reels[4] gives some idea of the old spectacular's mad charm.

A slapstick sequence begins with Pico chasing his hat. Fishing from bridge, he casts and hooks old woman. Goat butts Pico into water. Old Woman is hoisted by crane and falls out of her skirt.

A Room in the Haunted House

Pico and goat enter through window and go to sleep. When wakened, Pico sees boots walk up wall. He sees man seated reading newspaper, and pulls chair from under man. Man remains suspended in air. Pico tries it but falls. Man disappears through revolving door which is painted with bookcase on one side and china closet on other. Pico swings poker and breaks china. Covers fly off two other chairs and reveal two men. Pico orders them out and one disappears by diving through washstand. Other man drying hands on revolving towel on wall disappears hanging on to towel as it shoots through wall. Pico goes to sit down and chair slides up wall. Clock slides down wall and strikes him on head. Pico goes to sit on other chair and it flies out window. Gets ladder and as he is about to ascend, ladder shoots through wall.

The Haunted Bedroom

Pico kneels beside bed praying. Goat jumps through window and kneels beside Pico. He has trouble with contrary windows, opening and shutting. First comforter, then sheet and finally pillow fly through windows. As he sits on bed, mattress jumps up and down and then out the door. Skeleton appears at window. Girl enters room and advances to center of room. Pico slips his arm around her waist. Girl faces him and raises her large hat showing she is skeleton. Skeletons appear at windows. A porter enters dancing with huge trunk on his back. When Fantasma touches trunk it changes into an automobile. Pico and goat jump into auto and speed away.

The Witches Den

Scene changes to number of witches huddled around steaming cauldron over a fissure where flames and smoke shoot forth. The villain Zamaliel enters with ingenue Lena whom he hypnotizes. Then with Zamaliel making passes over her, she slowly rises and is seen reclining in midair without visible support. Zamaliel's lieutenants tell him they have failed to slay Pico. In a rage Zamaliel throws one into the smoking fissure and he disappears in the flames.

Temptation's Fountain

In a new scene, Zamaliel is tracking Lena's suitor Arthur along a road. Hidden behind shrubbery, Zamaliel conjures up a beautiful fountain composed of real people posing as statuary. Statues come to life in a tableau representing revelry. They are holding bunches of grapes, drinking from goblets. The pedestal slowly revolves and then stops. One statue gives Arthur a full goblet but he refuses.

The second tableau shows the statues around a large roulette wheel. Two statues are holding a horn of plenty filled with money. A statue spins the wheel and as it stops, money pours from the horn of plenty. They invite Arthur to gamble but he again refuses.

Statues in the third tableau are posed in alluring groups trying to entice Arthur. The nearest figure attempts to embrace him. He will not be tempted and continues his search for Lena. Zamaliel is in a rage and the fountain fades.

The Castle of Death

Pico and Goat are seen approaching the castle. When Pico raps on door, a knight in full armor comes out and marches off like an automaton. Inside is a dining table with two phantom knights who command Pico to sit. Pico raises cover of large dish beneath which are two lobsters. Lobsters stand up and appear to be fighting.

Knight places bottle and glass on the table. Bottle rises to fill Knight's glass. Bottle again fills knight's glass. Two more knights enter and do a clog dance. Pico imitates them and the scene becomes a prison cell.

Prison Cell

Pico is seized with fear and tries to escape. Knights block every door. Knight enters with head block. Headsman enters with large axe on his shoulder. Pico is trembling. First knight commands other knights to place Pico on block. Pico raises his head and asks knight by pantomime if he is going to cut off his head. Knight nods. Pico offers his finger instead.

Knight gives command and brings down axe heavily. Pico's head falls to floor. His arms and legs shake for few seconds. Knights place Pico's headless body on chair.

Fantasma appears and looks on Pico with pity. She picks up Pico's head and places it back on his shoulders.

The Dungeon Beneath the Sea

The characters enter the sea. Arthur is seen swimming to the bottom followed by Pico. At the bottom is a rocky background with a dungeon hewn in the rock. To the left is a huge octopus with feelers clinging to the rock. In the foreground is the stern of sunken galleon. Clinging to the ship's side are clams and oysters which open and close continuously. Large crabs and lobsters are crawling on the ocean bed.

Zamaliel drags Lena in and places her in the dungeon. He exits and Pico enters swimming. As he explores he feeds a fish to a clam and gets bitten. Two snakes appear from portholes and Pico battles them and a giant lobster. A Nondescript sneaks up and Pico engages it in a sword fight. Pico throws away his sword and rushes off. A swordfish darts across stage and runs his sword through the Nondescript's stomach.

Zamaliel enters with sprites who roll away the rock and bring out Lena. When she spurns his advances, he orders that she be destroyed by the octopus.

As Lena is being dragged, Arthur and Pico enter. Pico hides in fright but Arthur draws his sword to attack the sprites. Zamaliel calls for help and more sprites with swords appear. In a wild battle, Arthur kills them all and then attacks Zamaliel who unconsciously backs toward the octopus which seizes him in its feelers and strangles him to death. Pico comes out of hiding and poses victoriously over one of the bodies. The large shell opens revealing Fantasma.

Fantasma's Fairy Boat of Shells

Lena, Arthur and Pico are surrounded by Fantasma and her fairies. The boat is being drawn by mermaids, harnessed to the Fairy Boat by garlands of seaweed. The Fairy Boat is seen sailing nearer and nearer. The scene fades away.

The final scene is the trysting place where the story begins. Lena awakens Arthur from the spell and they embrace. A title frame announces that it was all only a dream.

George, Jr. continued with playwriting and his inventions, with two more spectacular effects patented in 1921 (see Appendix B). Along the way he teamed with Ferry Corwey, a European clown, in a vaudeville act, "The Hanlons." The team was engaged by Ed Wynn for comic invention for the 1937 musical *Hooray for What!* George resurrected and restaged the Haunted Hotel scene for a meeting of foreign delegates in Room 711 of the Grand Hôtel de L'Espionage. The old Hanlon magic worked. One critic said:

> The scene . . . crystallized the humor of those sets invented, we believe, by the Hanlons about the turn of the century[!] with sliding and turning panels and crazy doors through which the merry chase proceeded.
>
> Now it is a joyful task to report all this . . . we have been suffering so long from the absence of anything on the New York stage that would bring laughter from the very depths of your interior and split it in tornado-like gusts all through the house. This is not the kind of comedy that produces polite lip-merriment, or as you leave the theatre, "quite amusing." Instead, you will probably be incapable of any speech whatsoever.[5]

In George, Jr.'s version, there were 55 entrances and exits in seven minutes and "at least fourteen real laughs."

After the big shows closed around 1911, the old men—George, William and Edward—tried to keep busy in retirement with a variety of activities. George's wife, Helena, had died in 1911; William's wife, Clara, had died in 1892.

"Did you ever have any girls in your shows?" an interviewer asked. "We did have pretty girls—but it didn't do us much good," said Edward. "We always had our wives with us."

"That's a fact," added William. "We were all six married and we took our wives with us and were never happy without them."[6]

In the 1905 and 1907 programs for *Superba,* there is a line which credits Quincy Kilby for those versions of the play book. Kilby was well known to the Hanlons and was later employed to catalog Houdini's vast library. Through this connection, William came to know the great escape artist, and while Houdini was performing at the Hippodrome, they enjoyed dinners together, talking over show business and old times. Both men knew the thrill of performing daredevil feats.

Eventually, time caught up with the old men. William, very lonely, entered the Actors Home on Staten Island. First he had to transfer his annuity to the Actors Fund, since actors with funds of their own could not be provided for. Once he emerged and joined George and Edward to attend a matinee at the Park Theatre to see Alice Hanlon, Edward's daughter, star in *Erminie.*

Well over 80, William suddenly conceived the notion that he was a house painter of ability. As a result, there soon were fresh coats of paint on everything paintable at the Staten Island Home. William died on February 7, 1923, and was buried beside Clara in the cemetery near his beloved home in Cohasset.

George stayed for a time with a daughter in Detroit. Eventually he resided in the Home for the Aged, New York City. He died instantly when he stepped from between two parked cars on Amsterdam Avenue and was struck by a taxicab on November 5, 1926. His obituary lists his interment at Troy, New York.

Edward, the youngest, spent a few years in business in New York City and then retired to St. Petersburg, Florida. There he and his wife, Frances, celebrated their fiftieth wedding anniversary. They had been married in St. Petersburg, Russia. The last of the six remarkable brothers, Edward died in his sleep on March 8, 1931. He was survived by his wife, Frances, three daughters and one son.

CHAPTER TEN

~

In Conclusion

THE SAGA OF THE HANLON BROTHERS began with the boys performing acrobatic and gymnastic stunts, ever increasing in difficulty, to impress their audiences. Eventually with "Zampillaerostation" and the "Leap for Life," the young men reached the highest level of acrobatic prowess in their day. Purely physical stunts were the basis for their several world tours.

This exceptional physical skill stood the Hanlons in good stead when they segued into pantomime and became knockabout clowns. The brothers showed unusual aptitude for entertaining in dumb show, mixing comedy and acrobatic violence with outrageous plots. Now instead of merely doing tricks for their own sake, they captured audiences' minds with their phenomenal Parisian pantomimes and *Le Voyage en Suisse*. *Le Voyage* became an international hit.

When the Hanlons grew older and embarked on their producing career, they were entering the American theatre of popular culture. With *Fantasma*, and later with *Superba*, they chose a species of European *feerie* play with its struggle between good and evil. But they knew what made for good box office in this country, and they were conscious of some of the popular pantomimic successes that preceded them. The trick work of the Ravels and the silent clowning of George Fox in *Humpty-Dumpty* were echoed in the Hanlons' two "pantomimic spectaculars." These fairy stories were also augmented with non-sequitur variety acts.

About the time that *Superba* was at its zenith, the invention of motion pictures began to cast a shadow on the entertainment scene and would eventually have its profound effect on all show business.

For all its ingenuity, the 19th-century stage with its spectacles, melodrama and panoramas had to make way for the greater realism and flexibility of 20th-century film.[1] Twenty years after the nickelodeon appeared, the big Hanlon shows were no more.

From the beginning, George Méliès demonstrated the ease with which fantasy and astonishing tricks could be presented on the screen. On the dramatic stage, painted scenery and simulations of mountains, oceans, storms, chariot races and mob scenes could hardly compete with the real thing shown on film. Moreover, reels of film were cheaper to distribute than stage companies.

Of course, nothing could totally replace the real-time immediacy of live theatre. Musical comedy survived and flourished, and variety entertainment hung on into the 1920s. It was here that the second generation of Hanlons managed to continue their clowning.

The art of pantomime was preserved for a time because for the first 30 or more years, motion pictures were silent. Even with sub-titles, a large part of acting had to be mime. In particular, the silent film lent itself to the sight gag and physical comedy. Many of the early film comedians had learned their trade on the stage. Charlie Chaplin, Stan Laurel, Buster Keaton and others were long accustomed to silent acts and exhibiting every conceivable emotion. Later on, the Marx Brothers and the Three Stooges carried on the riotous nonsense and slapstick of the pantomimic clowns.

Long after the Hanlons' retirement, a conversation with the remaining brothers about the difference between modern shows and the Hanlon spectaculars was recorded in a newspaper interview.

"In our spectacular productions, we had hundreds of tricks—mechanical devices and feats of real cleverness. . . . But people don't want them nowadays," said William (who was the chief inventor of these trick props).

"No, they get effects in other ways. You spend lots of money on beautiful settings and costumes," said George. "And really, I'm not one of those who criticize modern tastes. Productions today are far more beautiful and artistic than we ever dreamed of making them. . . . But I think that we did have a little more cleverness at times. You see, we had to depend on our art alone to hold our audiences. We couldn't depend upon costumes or scenery. So we worked much harder and did more brain work."

"Do you suppose the public will ever want 'Superba' or 'Fantasma' again?" asked the interviewer.

The three old fellows looked at each other . . .

"Well I wonder," said Edward at last. "Just now, I think no one would care to see them—our ideas today are so different. And then—who could perform them?"[2]

~

The Hanlon vs. Agoust Feud

In *The New York Mirror* of February 18, 1888, the following article appeared, translated from a Paris periodical. It was apparently based on an interview with Henri Agoust. The story, somewhat abridged, was also published in *Acrobats and Mountebanks* by Hughes Le Roux and Jules Garnier (London, 1890). The authors claimed that Agoust told the account to them.

The History of the Hanlons.

Paris, Feb. 4, 1888

Agoust, who is now manager of the New Circus at Paris, pretends[1] that the book published under the title of "Memoirs of the Hanlon Brothers" is not the true history of the celebrated acrobats.

Agoust says that he first met the six Hanlon Brothers—Thomas, George, William, Alfred, Edward and Frederick—at Chicago about 1865. They were then performing as acrobats on the trapeze and on the carpet. Thomas and Albert, two splendidly-built fellows, were the "under men" in the pyramids. The other brothers were naturally thin and delicate. They have always worn two tights, a cheap one under the silk garment. To represent the muscles the under-tights were stuffed with long shreds of wool carefully combed, and one of the jokes used to be to stick pins mounted with white flags into these false mollets.

At Chicago the Hanlons did the vaulting while Agoust confined himself to juggling. Tanner was added with his dogs, and there was a female rope-dancer. However. the performance was too short and Agoust proposed to the Hanlons to add a pantomime. He taught them two old sketches, Harlequin Statue and Harlequin Skeleton. This experiment had great success, and in 1867 the troupe went to Paris and began its reputation with the pantomime of Village Saw Bones. The war of 1870 broke up the company. The Hanlons went to England with the Strandges troupe, which was then at the Chatelet, and Agoust joined the army. They met again in 1876, at the Walhalla in Berlin. The Hanlons were trying to mount a scene borrowed from the minstrel farce of Do, Mi, Sol, Do. They played as minstrels.

"What could you do in the piece?" they asked Agoust.

"You haven't any orchestra leader," he replied. "I will take my place at the music stand."

And the five Hanlons admitted this former companion in their fortune to replace their brother Thomas who had died in America. Thomas had fallen at Cincinnati, one evening and cut open his head while making a leap. He had been doctored as well as possible, but he suffered atrocious pains when the brothers jumped upon his mended head. He cried: "I won't do it. I can't stand it any longer!"

"Coward! lazy devil!" replied George, the terrible man of the band.

And he inspired so much fear that the unfortunate Thomas continued to perform and in a few months he became crazy.

Agoust says that the Hanlon Brothers were hard and merciless workers. They rehearsed every day except Sunday from ten in the morning until two, and from four in the afternoon until six. When they were tired of leaping they would sit down and work mentally.

"My boys, don't ever drink before the performance," said George. "After you can do as you like."

Do, Mi, Sol, Do had an extraordinary success at the Folies Bergere. The Hanlons had been engaged for a month at a salary of $1,800. The evening of the first performance they signed an engagement at $3,000 a month and played their pantomime thirteen months running. This piece and Le Voyage en Suisse met with great favor in Belgium and England. In this latter country, Agoust left the Hanlons.

The following heated response from the Hanlons appeared in the February 25 issue of *The New York Mirror.* It is notable for its exceptional vehemence and some departures from other records of the Hanlon history.

The Hanlons and Agoust.

Last week we published a letter from our Paris correspondent which contained an account by Agoust, manager of the New Circus in the French capital, of his alleged experience with the well-known Hanlon Brothers some years ago. The statements were called forth in connection with the history of this family written by the private secretary of Victor Hugo and printed in France. It seems that Agoust's remarks were actuated by malice, he having cherished a grudge of long standing against the Hanlons. The latter make the following vigorous statement in answer to the man's assertions:

New York, Feb. 21, 1888

DEAR SIR: It is a thankless and most ungracious duty to be compelled to defend one's personal character from the malignancy, mendacity and ingratitude of a self-convicted liar. The character of the wretched ghoul, who fattens on the grave, and on the absent, where he is known would require at our hands no answer to venomous slanders; but the mendacious article appearing in your reputable and well-read journal gives tone and leads a vraisemblance [sic] that might leave on its perusal some misshapen and distorted prejudice which we reluctantly stoop to answer and arrest.

After the unfortunate fall of Thomas, while performing at Cincinnati, we determined amicably to divide our company into two; the management of one being under Thomas, Edward and Frederick Hanlon, and the other under George, William and Alfred. We never after reunited. Thomas subsequently became the lessee of Wood's Theater, New York, Charles D. Brown being his associate partner and business manager. Afterward Thomas and Dr. Brown made the tour of the United States, then to Europe playing brilliant engagements in London and Paris. While in the latter city he [Thomas] joined the American circus under Mr. David Bidwell, the popular and well-known manager of the St. Charles and other theatres in New Orleans. This Parisian engagement was during the splendid international exposition of the empire.

After leaving Paris, Thomas, the senior brother, organized in Europe a powerful and accomplished company and returned to the United States, under the business management of the well-known dramatic agent, Maurice Simmonds, of 116 Broadway. It was during the close of the season that the sudden and appalling disappearance of Thomas from the company gave the family the first intimation of that mental aberration so painful in its results. This unhappy disaster happened three years after the unfortunate calamity in Cincinnati. Mr. Bidwell, Dr. Charles D. Brown, of No. 164 West Twenty-third street, a gentleman whose professional attainments was recognized throughout the scientific world and whose exalted rank in Freemasonry is the highest evidence of merit and character, and Mr. Maurice Simmonds, as well as the profession at large are all sufficiently familiar with the facts to flatly and indignantly refute the vile aspersions of Agoust and give the lie direct to his base and infamous insinuations.

It is extremely absurd to gravely answer the ridiculous charge that Agoust taught us pantomime when we were all bearded men, after a life time of active professional labor. We began as pantomimists as children, appearing in Cinderella and the juvenile pantomimes. After the death of Professor John Lees we joined the Chearini and Nicolo Circus and Pantomime company in Havana long before any of us attained majority and were active and laboring members of the company.

It was a serious misfortune for us to mount a pantomime in America at the greedy solicitation of Agoust. We committed the egregious blunder of permitting him to play the part of Pierrot, and his complete and mortifying failure compelled its speedy withdrawal. "There *was* a female rope dancer," to use his unmanly and coarse slur on his own wife, attached to the company. Her real name was Mrs. Agoust, the wife of Agoust, whose base insinuations violates the decencies of married as well as professional life.

It was our misfortune to have this swollen toad of vanety [sic], conceit, cowardice and immorality upon our hands three years in Europe, and a short time in the United States. He held subordinate positions in our company here, taking parts to which we might assign him after instruction and he was never admitted to our confidence, responsibility, duties, nor even our respect. We at length dismissed him in disgrace from our troupe for his grossly immoral and unscrupulous conduct—the noisome scandal of which was known to all Paris through the grave charges published in *Figaro* which Agoust was compelled to recall or suppress or quit the company he had mortified and disgraced instanter.

We learn though we have not seen the article, that the *Courier des Etats Unis,* of recent publication, has another article from the mendacious Agoust. Should it in any way attack our personal or professional reputation we shall promptly answer it. If it but contains a rehash of his absurd and laughable insinuations we shall unceremoniously dismiss them with silent contempt.

HANLON BROTHERS

Agoust's rebuttal appearing in the April 28 issue of *The New York Mirror* is exceptionally calm in tone given the vituperation of the Hanlons' attack.

Letter to the Editor.

HENRI AGOUST DEFENDS HIMSELF.

Nouveau Cirque
Paris, April 3, 1888

DEAR SIR—Availing myself of my fair right of reply, I must call on you to insert the following letter in rejoinder to the unseeming communication from the Hanlon Brothers published in your number of February 17 [sic] and which has but now come to my attention.

The Hanlon Brothers charge me with having made a failure of the role of Pierrot which according to their statement, I am asserted to have played with them in a pantomime, put on the stage, as they admit, in accordance with my advice. But it appears by programmes in my possession that in this production Pierrot was played by William Hanlon and Halegain [sic] by George. I had reserved for myself the part of Leander (The Marquis).

The Hanlons assert that before making my acquaintance they had studied pantomime in the course of their performance of Cinderella, an assertion which discredits them in the minds of all people who have any knowledge of the facts. There are in Cinderella really but two parts—the maiden and the prince—both played by young girls. The other parts are taken by children recruited for each occasion from the town where the representation is given.

As for the share my professional skill had in the final success of the Hanlons I can cite figures which speak louder than words. When in 1877, I met the Hanlons in Berlin, the entire troupe—comprising eight persons in all—the five brothers, a pupil, and Mmes. Frederic and Alfred Hanlon—had been engaged by M. Dussel for the Walhalla at a total monthly salary of 3,500 francs. The first month of my appearance with the company the salary went up to 5,000 francs. Two months later it touched 6,000 and then progressively rose to 7,000 and 8,000. In Paris we went to the Folies Bergeres with an engagement for a month at 9,000 francs and engagement renewed for a year at 15,000 francs a month. When it was proposed to go to the Theatre des Varietes to bring out Le Voyage en Suisse the Hanlons tried to leave me out of their bargain but the director required that I should be present at, should concur in, and sign the contract.

The charge of immorality brought against me I can settle with one word. The divorce from my first wife was granted *me* in America. As I cannot allow an accusation of this sort to be kept hanging over me, I have brought a libel suit against the Hanlons in the French courts, which will at the same time render a decision on the fair usage in cases of partnerships dissolved by one of the parties without proper accounting and settlement.

I close by reasserting the scrupulous correctness of the notice in the *Temps* concerning my relations with the Hanlons.

Thanking you, Mr. Editor for the publicity you are kind enough to give my letter, I remain very truly yours.

HENRI AGOUST
Regisseur-General de Nouveau Cirque

The duel in the public prints ceased with this letter in the May 12 issue of
The New York Mirror.

FINAL WORDS FROM THE HANLONS.

Manchester, N.H. May 4, 1888

Dear Sir—In your issue of April 3 [sic] appears an article concerning ourselves,
by Henri Agoust, which seems to require some notice from us though the character of its author, to those who know him, would be a sufficient answer.

He says that he has brought an action of libel against us in the French
courts. This is the first that we have ever heard of such proceedings and are unaware that it is possible that we could be sued in a foreign court without any notice of any kind or description. If any such suit exists we shall be pleased to meet
it anywhere. In our previous letter we did not enter into his divorce proceedings,
and his divorce procured in Chicago against his wife in France can hardly have
cleared him from the gross scandal which occurred at the Folies Bergeres [sic].
With regard to his notice in the *Temps* in which he said there was an effort to as-
sassinate him by the falling of a mirror upon him and by a rap of unusual sever-
ity with the barometer in the course of one of our plays the charge is too silly to
require an answer to anyone who has ever seen Le Voyage en Suisse.

With regard to the charge that our brother Thomas, after his fall in Cincinnati was compelled by gross abuse and threats of George Hanlon to continue
performances while his injuries were unhealed and until he became insane, the
reply is conclusive that his fall in Cincinnati was about three years prior to his
showing any indications of insanity, that George was never with him at the latter time and had not been for upwards of two years, that he had fully recovered
from his injuries in Cincinnati and had personally managed enterprises of his
own in America, England and France and was at the time en tour of the United
States and associated in the management with Morris Simmonds, of New York.

It is certainly very unpleasant to be called upon to defend ourselves against
such outrageous falsities and by a man whom we were compelled to get rid of
years ago, and who through the public prints has attempted to obtain some no-
toriety and to vent an otherwise ineffectual spite. We certainly shall pay no more
attention to him and feel that in the minds of those who know us no further notice is required.

HANLON BROTHERS

Hanlon Patents

Velocipedes

U.S. Patent No. 79,654, July 7, 1868. Improvement in Velocipedes. George, William, Alfred, Edward and Frederick Hanlon.

The Hanlons found the velocipedes imported from France and England (shown in patent fig. 4, opposite) to be heavy and impossible to adjust for riders of different size.

Their patent offered a new design which made the seat adjustable on an inclined frame and the length of the foot pedals on the front axle also adjustable so that the whole apparatus might be used by either large or small persons (see patent fig. 1).

As the illustrations show, the invention also hangs the rear axle on a forked rear end of the frame so that either one or two wheels may be mounted on it. Persons learning to ride could use two rear wheels, while experts would use only one wheel on each of the two axles (see patent figs. 2 and 3).

The patent states that the wheels may have rubber rings around the tires to make them noiseless and prevent them from slipping.

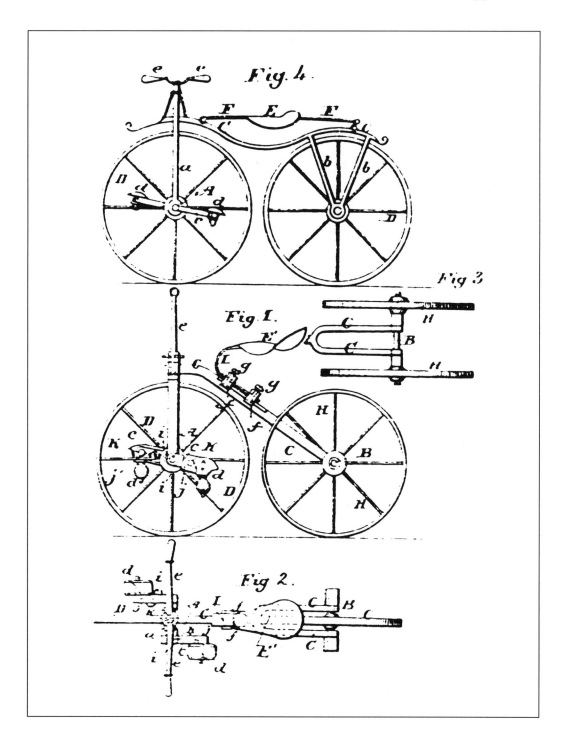

U.S. Patent No. 86,834, February 9, 1869. IMPROVEMENT IN VELOCIPEDES. William Hanlon and four brothers.

William added a shield over the front wheel to protect the rider's clothing during turns and to further protect the rider during spills by limiting the rotation of the front wheel. It sometimes happened that the rider, losing control, had his leg caught between the wheel and the frame and risked being severely injured.

Some previous velocipedes had a brake on the rear wheel operated by the rider leaning back in the saddle. Another of William's improvements provided a brake on the front wheel, operating it by a mechanism controlled by the steering handles. (See patent figs. 3 and 4.)

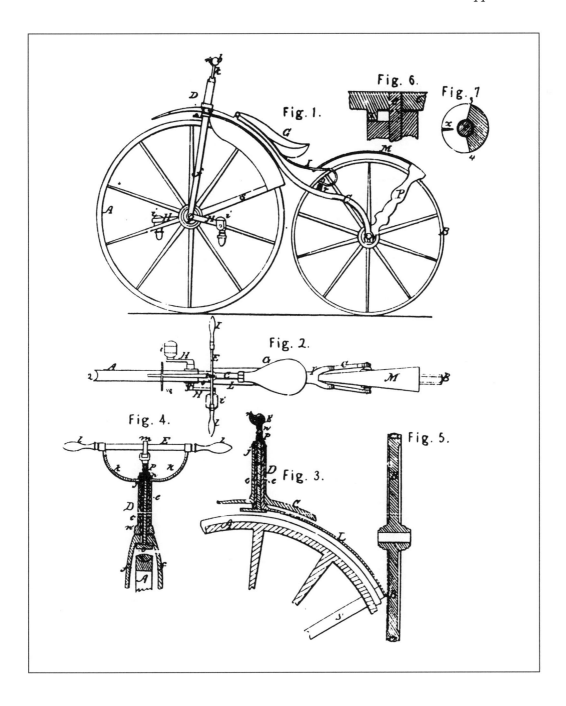

Theatrical Boat Scenery

U.S. Patent No. 263,900, September 5, 1882. THEATRICAL SCENERY AND APPLIANCES. W. Hanlon.

This complex stage scenery produces the effect of a ship in dock, leaving the dock, passing out of the harbor and finally at sea in rough water. This is accomplished by moving the scenery at the wings which are slid back while the ship remains in place. The moving scenery may also be operated by rotating the view on massive rollers like a diorama.

In stormy waters, the boat rocks realistically. Once at sea, the stern of the ship opens up to expose a salon, staterooms, etc., where a party is in progress. The action of the actors and the Hanlons' acrobatic stunts in a wildly pitching scene are described in Chapter Four.

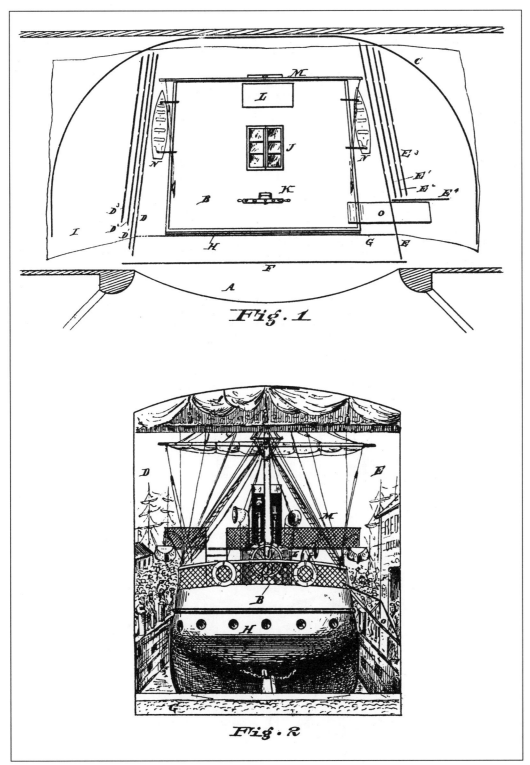

Fig.1

Fig.2

Continued.

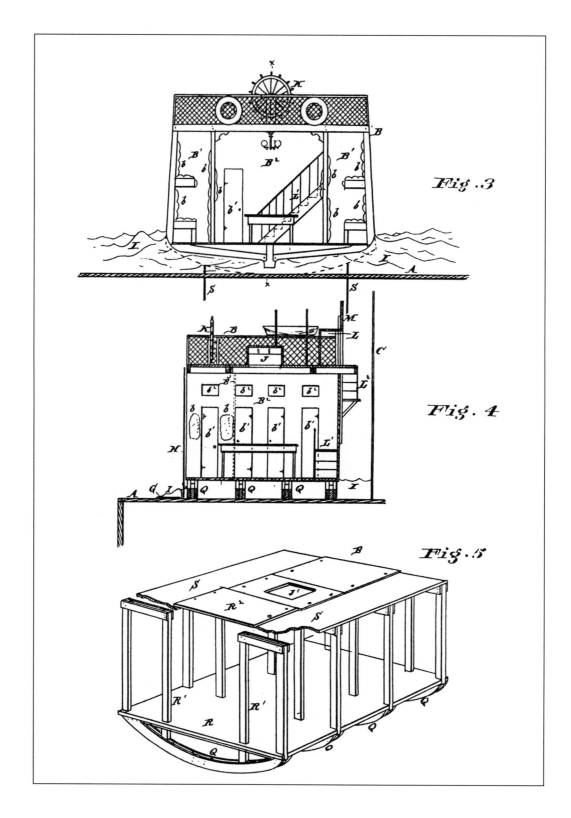

Fig. 3

Fig. 4

Fig. 5

Ludicrous Pantomimic Representations

U.S. Patent No. 293,324, February 12, 1884. THEATER APPLIANCE. William Hanlon.

Patent specifications state that this invention may be adapted to theatrical, circus or pantomimic performances, or for street parades to obtain a comical effect.

As shown in patent fig. 2, an imitation horse's head is secured on the hind quarters of the horse. The rider's face is covered with a mask and a duplicate mask is placed at the back of his head and the two covered with a single comical hat. To the man's back is secured a padding representing another body to which is secured an imitation pair of legs. The coat has two pairs of sleeves. Reins are placed in the rider's hands and also that of the dummy. A double saddle and ornamental bands hide the juncture of the dummy horse head with the real horse.

On the stage the effect of this device is very ludicrous. If the horse backs, the effect is as if the animal were moving properly in one direction; the same is true in the other direction; but during such movements it appears as if the two horses and two men were trying to ride out of each other or trying to effect a separation.

The patent notes that any animal with two heads may be used, such as an elephant or giraffe. The concept is applicable to fowl or birds, and in place of a man or figure of a man, another animal, such as a monkey, may be used.

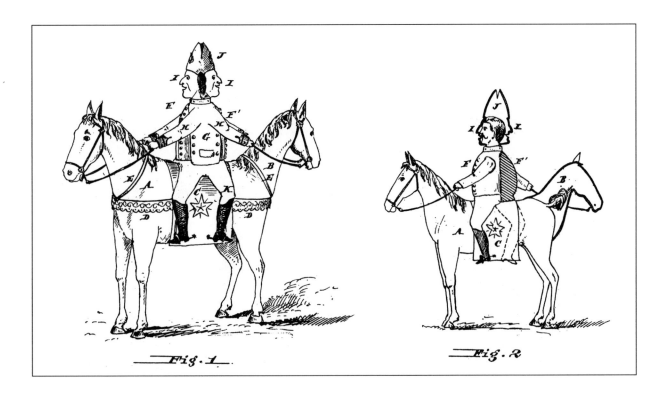

Beheading Block and Ax

U.S. Patent No. 420,995, February 11, 1890. BEHEADING BLOCK AND AX. William Hanlon.

This invention produces an illusive beheading on stage under full light, so realistic that as the victim's head lies upon the block and the descending ax and block give forth the natural thud of a blow, the blade appears to actually sever the neck. The body falls to the floor and the head falls through the block to an opening in the base at a distance from its natural position.

As can be seen in the patent illustrations, the blade of the ax has a concave edge which is covered by sheet rubber so that the blade appears to be a single piece of metal. It can be swung forcefully and the edges strike the block without harming the victim.

The victim's neck rests on a rubber trap so that the victim can fall forward with his head inside the block. This action releases a dummy head which falls to the floor and can be seen through the open sides of the block. The apparently beheaded victim can imitate the contortions of death.

This illusion was introduced in *Fantasma* in 1895, with Pico the clown acting as the victim.

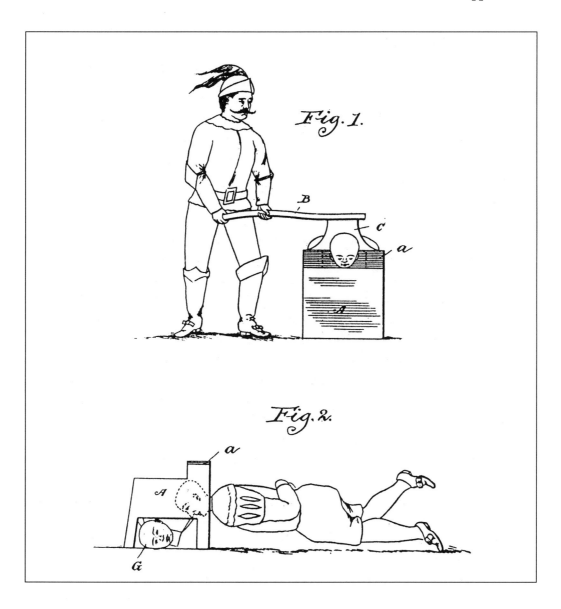

Dismembering Apparatus

U.S. Patent No. 421,493, February 18, 1890. DISMEMBERING APPARATUS. William Hanlon.

This invention provides the illusion of severing all the limbs and head of a human from the trunk in full view of the audience under full light.

In performance, an actor in a vengeful mood approaches a seated knight, swinging a sword and uttering threats. The intended victim is making natural movements with his legs, arms, head and face, and some movements of the hands and arms, apparently in an effort to prevent the actor from cutting off his legs, which the actor proceeds to do, leaving bloody stumps and setting the legs aside. The actor then severs the right arm, which drops to the floor, and then repeats the action with the victim's left arm. Both arms on the floor continue to flail about.

The actor then, after some byplay, approaches the knight to sever his head. During the severing operations, the knight makes faces and ridicules the actor but as the sword passes between the body and the head of the knight he can only make some guttural noises. Immediately the head rises well above the trunk. The actor draws a curtain in front of the dismembered knight and walking across the stage boasts of his feat. In the midst of this, the knight, fully reassembled, enters and walks in front of the actor and exits.

In the patent illustrations, Fig. 1 shows the knight seated in his chair. Figs. 2 and 3 show the arrangement of four persons behind the scene necessary to accomplish the illusion. The body of the knight is a dummy. A man on each side provides an arm, projected through the scene. A man lying on his back provides the legs and eventually the bloody knee stumps. The fourth man, standing in a stooped position, supplies the head. When the head is severed, he straightens up and the head rises as shown in patent fig. 4.

There have been a variety of dismemberment illusions performed by stage magicians over the years. This one appeared in *Superba* about 1894, with Pierrot playing the part of the knight.

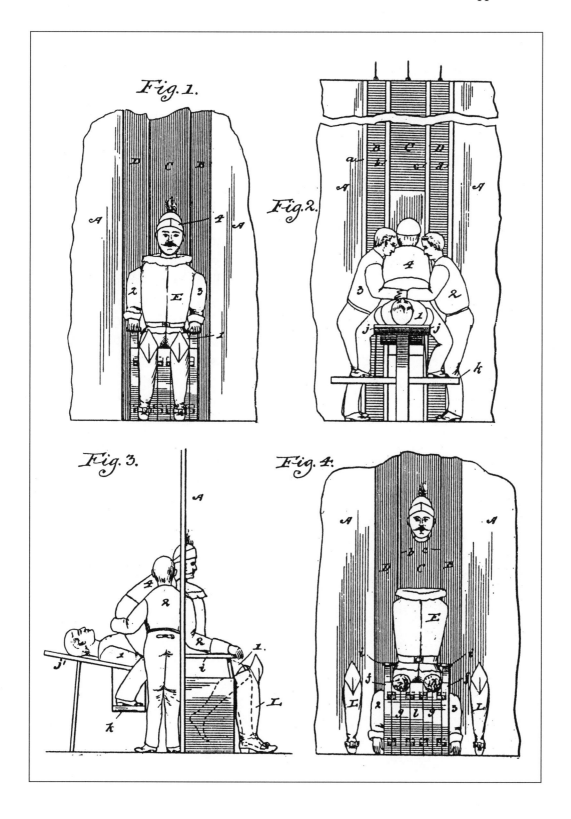

Fig. 1.

Fig. 2.

Fig. 3.

Fig. 4.

Conjuring Apparatus

U.S. Patent No. 554,682, February 18, 1896. CHAIRS FOR VANISHING. William Hanlon.

This patent covers a variety of chairs constructed so that a subject can be concealed in the hollow interior of the chair in a deceptive manner. Figs. 1, 2 and 3 of the patent illustrations show Hanlon's preferred model introduced in *Superba* about 1894.

The "Execution Chair," sitting on a platform, is carried onto the stage. The condemned girl is seated and the platform raised to the shoulders of four men, who stand downstage at the footlights. A hood is thrown over the girl. The good fairy appears to rescue her. The hood is thrown back and the girl has vanished.

The four feet of the chair and platform are hollow. When the hood is lowered, the subject places her legs into the two front legs of the chair (and platform). Then she lays her body down upon the seat of the chair so as to be received into the seat compartment and thrusts her arms down into the compartments formed by the two rear legs of the chair. A hinged door closes the seat compartment so that she cannot be seen when the hood is raised.

This proved to be a very puzzling trick and immensely popular with *Superba* audiences. Most reviewers singled it out for favorable comment.

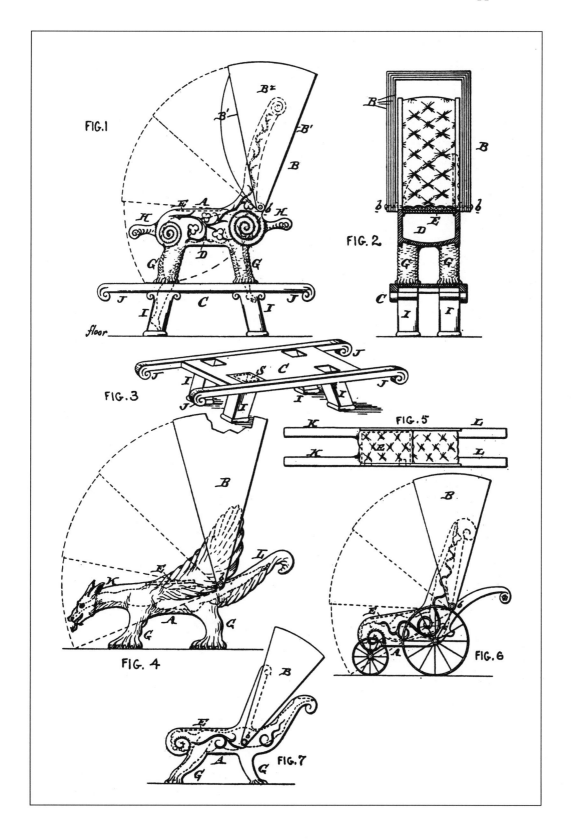

Theatrical Illusion Apparatus

U.S. Patent No. 1,035,435, August 13, 1912. Magic Production Box. William Hanlon.

A box approximately six feet in length is brought in and rested on trestles to isolate it from the stage floor. A door on the end of the box is opened and a second box completely filling the original box is slid out. The original box is now stood on end and two front doors opened for a subject to step out.

This patent provides for a sturdy, collapsible box to be secreted in the double walls of the original box. This second box springs open immediately as it is being slid out. The subject is in her compartment from the beginning.

The mechanism for the expanding box is intricate and practical, but it is questionable whether an audience would find the effect particularly mystifying. This patent was granted about the same time the Hanlon shows ceased to tour.

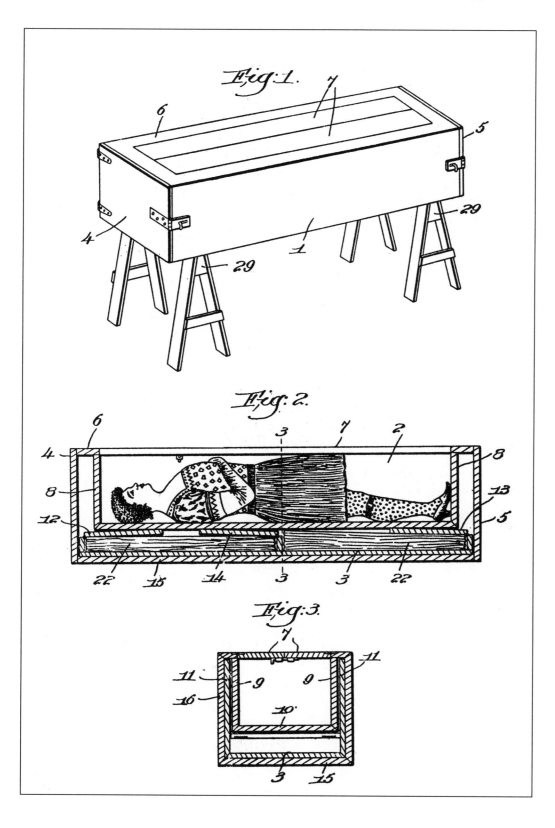

Fig. 1.

Fig. 2.

Fig. 3.

Means for Producing Theatrical Stage Effects

George W. Hanlon, Jr., son of George Hanlon, patented three mechanisms for spectacular stage effects.

U.S. Patent No. 883,953, April 7, 1908. GIANT SOAP BUBBLE. G. W. Hanlon.

Several stationary hoops or rings are mounted on a rotary platform. The hoops are variously colored. When the platform is rotated rapidly, a transparent, spherical shape is formed, creating the effect of a large soap bubble. A stationary platform inside the bubble accommodates a dancer or other performance. The rotating mechanism is, of course, hidden from the audience.

This was premiered in *Fantasma* and later in a variety sketch which occasioned the writing of the song, "I'm Forever Blowing Bubbles."

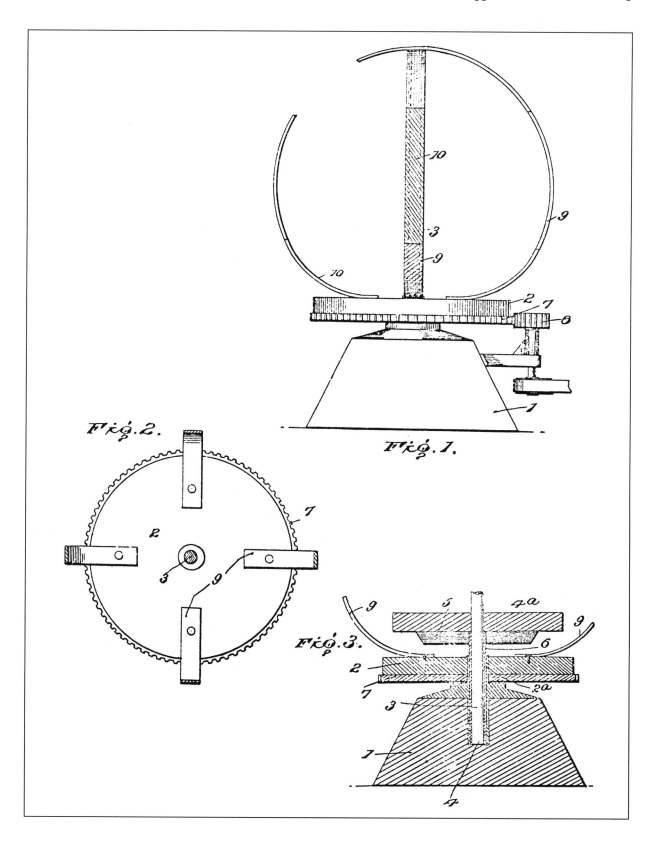

Fig.2.

Fig.1.

Fig.3.

U.S. Patent No. 1,365,989, January 18, 1921. Transparent Star. G. W. Hanlon.

This patent is similar to the "bubble" patent, but a six-pointed, transparent star is created on a more portable mechanism.

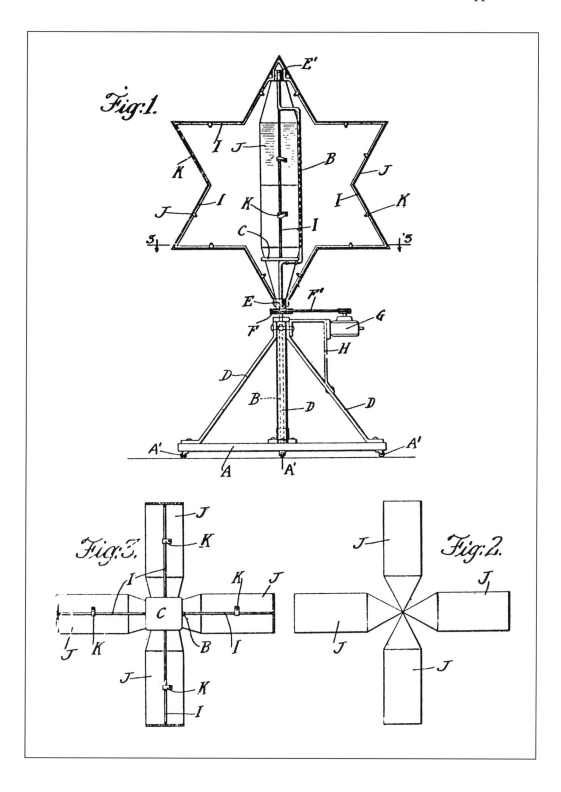

Fig:1.

Fig:3.

Fig:2.

U.S. Patent No. 1,365,990, January 18, 1921. GIANT JEWEL. G. W. Hanlon.

Highly polished vanes, some colored, rotate and counter-rotate under brilliant light to simulate a jewel. A performer may appear inside the gem.

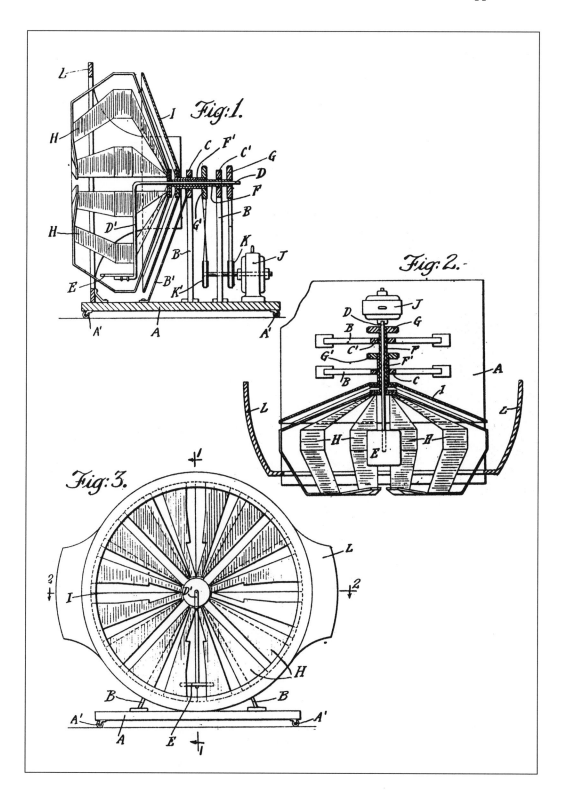

Notes

An Important Note to the Reader

1. Alfred's birth date was unrecorded, but his date of christening was February 5, 1843.
2. Frederick was an adopted child. No Manchester baptism is recorded.

Acknowledgments and Sources

1. M. Willson Disher, *Clowns & Pantomimes*, London, 1925, page 156.

CHAPTER ONE. *The First Ten Years Around the World*

1. *Mémoires et Pantomimes des Frères Hanlon-Lees.*
2. "Half a Century an Acrobat," an unidentified Boston newspaper feature, c. 1909.
3. *Mémoires.*
4. Playbills in the Harvard Theatre Collection.
5. Thomas Walton, "Entortilationists," in *Life and Letters Today*, April 1941. See the playbill for the debut.
6. *Mémoires.*
7. Ibid.
8. Ibid.
9. *Pittsburgh Leader*, December 24, 1911.
10. Interview with William in an unidentified newspaper.
11. *Mémoires.*
12. Ibid.

CHAPTER TWO. *From 1856 to "Zampillaerostation"*

1. *Mémoires.*
2. *Pittsburgh Gazette*, December 24, 1911.
3. An unidentified newspaper, October 16, 1887.
4. *Mémoires.*

5. *The New York Times*, December 3, 1905.

6. From the Italian *zampillare* (to spring forth).

7. Description adapted from *The New York Clipper*, December 21, 1861.

8. *Mémoires.*

9. See Figure 5.

10. Ibid.

CHAPTER THREE. *1865–1869: Tragedy and a Change of Course*

1. *Mémoires.*

2. Ibid.

3. An acrobat inside a large ball causes it to ascend a spiral ramp.

4. An unidentified newspaper, January 21, 1896.

5. *Mémoires.*

6. An unidentified newspaper, January 3, 1911.

7. Ibid.

8. In some accounts, the Dan Costello Circus; in others, the John Robinson Circus.

9. An unidentified newspaper, January 21, 1896.

10. An unidentified newspaper, November 25, 1869.

11. Letter from William to C. A. Brown, January 21, 1870, Baltimore, in the Harvard Theatre Collection.

CHAPTER FOUR. *Pantomime from 1870*

1. Doctor Judd, "Fifty Years Recollections," *Billboard*, December 5, 1903.

2. Condensed from *Mémoires.*

3. Thomas Walton, "Entortilationists," in *Life and Letters Today*, April–June 1941.

4. Condensed from *Mémoires.*

5. Translated and condensed from a review in *Le Tintamarre*, November 3, 1878.

6. Translated and condensed from *Le Temps*, October 21, 1878, and *L'Événement*, October 21, 1878.

7. Georges Moynet, *Trucs et Décor*, Paris, c. 1880.

8. *Journal Quotidien*, Paris, September 10, 1885.

9. Georges Moynet, op. cit.

10. Silent Mora, quoted by John Braun in *The Linking Ring*, April 1957.

11. A. A. Hopkins (comp.), *Magic*, New York, 1897, p. 50.

CHAPTER FIVE. *1879: Le Voyage en Suisse*

1. John H. Towsen, *Clowns*, New York, 1976.

2. Preface by Theodore Banville to *Mémoires*, Paris, 1879.

3. Émile Zola, "La Pantomime," in *Le Naturalisme au Théâtre*, 1881.

4. L. Wingfield, *Theatre*, May 1, 1880.

5. Chaos in the dining room was the Hanlons' version of the famous Price Brothers' sketch *An Evening at Maxims*.

6. This last stunt, which had been used in the "shipwreck" scene described in Chapter Four, was possible only because the dining room table was covered by a sheet of rubber.

7. L. Wingfield, op. cit.

8. Émile Zola, op cit.

9. *Standard*, March 29, 1880.

10. An unidentified newspaper, October 16, 1887.

11. *Illustrated Sporting & Dramatic News*, April 17, 1880.

12. This accusation was originally published in *Le Temps*, date uncertain. See Appendix A.

13. *Spirit of the Times*, March 27, 1880.

CHAPTER SIX. *1884: Fantasma*

1. See descriptions in A. Nicholas Vardac, *Stage to Screen*, Cambridge, 1949.

2. *Spirit of the Times*, November 15, 1884.

3. *The New York Clipper*, November 22, 1884.

4. Ibid.

5. G. D. C. Odell, *Annals of the New York Stage*, vol. XII, 1927–49, p. 440.

6. *The New York Clipper*, November 22, 1884.

7. Ibid.

8. "Christmas Eve in the Wings," *Boston Globe*, December 25, 1888.

9. Ibid.

10. *Boston Globe*, December 23, 1888.

11. *Boston Globe*, December 1888.

12. *Sunday Herald* (Boston), September 9, 1906.

CHAPTER SEVEN. *1890: Superba*

1. *The New York Times*, November 25, 1890.

2. Ibid.

3. Article by Fred Hanlon in an unidentified newspaper, date unknown.

4. Silent Mora, *Magic, Mirth, Mystery, The Sphinx*, December 1944.

5. Theatre review, *Chicago Inter Ocean*, September 9, 1894.

6. *Toledo Time*, February 22, 1908.

7. A Cleveland newspaper, October 24, 1892.

8. Theatre review, *Chicago Inter Ocean*, 1897.
9. Article by Fred Hanlon in an unidentified newspaper, date unknown.
10. Newspaper account, January 2, 1906.
11. Review of *Fantasma* at Alhambra, in an unidentified newspaper.
12. Review of *Fantasma, Pittsburgh Leader*, November 8, 1906.
13. *Syracuse Post*, April 5, 1910.

CHAPTER NINE. *The Later Years*

1. *Atlanta Journal*, February 21, 1911.
2. Interview with Fred Hanlon in an unidentified newspaper, c. 1918.
3. Review with cast, *New York Dramatic Mirror*, December 9, 1914.
4. Abridged from a script in the Boston Public Library, Rare Books Department.
5. Review by Sidney B. Whipple of opening at New York Winter Garden, in a New York newspaper, 1937.
6. *Boston Sunday Post*, March 20, 1921.

CHAPTER TEN. *In Conclusion*

1. This transition is brilliantly covered by A. Nicholas Vardac in *Stage to Screen*, Cambridge, 1949.
2. *Boston Sunday Post*, March 20, 1921.

APPENDIX A. *The Hanlon vs. Agoust Feud*

1. Probably "contends."

GAYLORD F